Championship Sambo
Submission Holds and Groundfighting

Championship Sambo
Submission Holds and Groundfighting

By Steve Scott

Turtle Press   .   Hartford

CHAMPIONSHIP SAMBO: SUBMISSION HOLDS AND GROUNDFIGHTING

To contact the author or to order additional copies of this book:
call 1-800-778-8785 or visit www.TurtlePress.com

ISBN 9781880336908
LCCN 2006011678
Printed in the United States of America

10 9 8 7 6 5 4 3 2 1 0

Warning-Disclaimer

This book is designed to provide information on specific skills used in the sport of sambo, also known as sombo. It is not the purpose of this book to reprint all the information that is otherwise available to the author, publisher, printer or distributors, but instead to compliment, amplify and supplement other texts. You are urged to read all available material, learn as much as you wish about the subjects covered in this book and tailor the information to your individual needs. Anyone practicing the skills presented in this book should be physically capable to do so and have the permission of a licensed physician before participating in this activity or any physical activity.

Every effort has been made to make this book as complete and accurate as possible. However, there may be mistakes, both typographical and in content. Therefore, this text should be used only as a general guide and not the ultimate source of information on the subjects presented here in this book on sambo or any skill or subject. The purpose of this book is to provide information and entertain. The author, publisher, printer and distributors shall neither have liability nor responsibility to any person or entity with respect to loss or damages caused, or alleged to have been caused, directly or indirectly, by the information contained in this book.

Library of Congress Cataloguing in Publication Data

Scott, Steve, 1952-
Championship sambo : submission holds and groundfighting / by Steve Scott.
    p. cm.
ISBN-13: 978-1-880336-90-8
ISBN-10: 1-880336-90-1
1. Sambo wrestling. I. Title.
GV1197.5.S36 2006
796.812--dc22   2006011678

Acknowledgements

Thanks to the following people for appearing in the photos used in this book: Becky Scott, Jan Trussell, Chris Heckadon, Shawn Watson, Bill West, Eric Millsap, Warren Frank, Kenney Brink and Bob Rittman. Photography: Steve Scott, Bill West, Bob Rittman, Chuck Lance, Holly Weddington and Eric Millsap. Technical Support: Bob Rittman

Contents

INTRODUCTION

Almost every culture on this planet has its own system of wrestling or fighting and it was the culture of the Soviet Union that gave birth to the rugged sport of sambo. There have been few books written on this subject and with sambo's recent surge in popularity, it is a good time to offer a serious, technical look at the Russian martial sport that has changed the way the martial arts world looks at grappling. This book will focus in on the groundfighting skills that have made sambo so unique. While sambo's approach to throws and takedowns is also unique, it is my intention to provide some comprehensive and realistic grappling skills in this volume. But I hope to convey more than only the mechanical tools of this great sport and martial art. Sambo is more than a bunch of techniques mixed together to see which works best. It's a whole way of looking at grappling and wrestling that emphasizes efficiency over aesthetics and victory over defeat.

Sambo was born in the old Soviet Union and its roots are steeped in the social fabric of one of the most brutal regimes in history. It's a sport that either makes the best out of you or takes the best from you.

Sambo's technical theories are based on Kodokan Judo and an objective look at history proves that statement. Vasili Oshchepekov, the man who initially developed what became known as sambo, trained in Japan under judo's founder Jigoro Kano. Oshchepekov didn't hide the fact that judo was the basis for the new form of grappling combat he developed and he lost his life for it. A victim of Stalin's purges in the late 1930s, Oshchepekov was killed for being a Japanese sympathizer because of the credit he gave judo for sambo's early technical development.

While judo was the initial martial discipline that Oshchepekov studied, he and his comrades traveled across the Soviet Union taking the best they could find from the many regional wrestling styles they encountered. And, as with any human activity, sambo evolved and took on a personality all its own. Eventually, sambo was the primary style of wrestling a promising youngster would take up in the Soviet Union. As the child grew and developed, he might be able to train in the Olympic sports of judo, freestyle wrestling or Greco-Roman wrestling. He might also have stayed in the primary sport, sambo, and pursued his athletic career in this native wrestling style of the Soviet Union. Whichever he chose, or was directed to choose, it was sambo that was his primary wrestling and grappling education.

In this book, we take a comprehensive look at the submission techniques that make sambo unique. These are the armlocks and leglocks that make up much of what sambo is. We will also look at the holds and breakdowns that make sambo so effective in ground wrestling. As mentioned later on in this book, sambo took the world by storm in the 1960s and forever changed how people teach judo, wrestling, jujitsu and any form of grappling. Sambo has proven its worth in the world of mixed martial arts and sambo wrestlers are very successful in this form of competition.

This book is the result of years of training and coaching and comes from my perspective as an American coach and sambo wrestler. Sambo's history in the United States is a colorful one and I was around for many of its early years. From my point of view, sambo in the United States is as good as anywhere in the world and the skills presented here have all been tested on competitive mats around the world.

I would like to thank Becky Scott, who, besides being my best friend and a very patient wife, is one of America's all-time great sambo champions. She retired undefeated after winning the Pan American Games and World Championship in 1983. Her advice and counsel during the writing of this book are appreciated. Along with Becky, my friends Jim Schneweis, Bob Corwin and John Saylor influenced me profoundly for many years. These men are the best coaches I know and it's been a pleasure and honor working with them.

Many thanks to Becky Scott, Chris Heckadon, Shawn Watson, Bill West, Eric Milsap, Jan Trussell, Kenney Brink, Warren Frank and Bob Rittman for their help. These people are gifted athletes and technicians and their skill is what you see in the pages of this book.

My gratitude and respect go to Maurice Allen, the Scotsman who was my first sambo coach and Ken Regennitter, my judo coach and the person who suggested to me that I give sambo a try. I'm glad I listened to Ken's advice.

Finally, I want to dedicate this book to Dr. Ivan Olsen, the father of American Sambo. Ivan was my mentor, and the mentor to many sambo wrestlers and coaches in the United States. He was the Chairman of the AAU (Amateur Athletic Union) Sambo Committee for many years and responsible for the early growth of the sport in the United States. Ivan was a great wrestling coach and leader, but an even greater human being. Many of us owe him a lot.

The skills presented in this book have all passed the tests of both time and competition. There is no filler or fluff here. Everything presented has been used successfully in all levels of competitive sambo. I am a firm believer that fundamentally sound skills performed by a motivated and well-conditioned wrestler who has molded what he knows to work for him with a high ratio of success is hard to beat. This is the approach I have taken as an athlete and as a coach and I hope to convey that to you in this book as well. Sambo is a real test of fitness, skill and courage. It is my belief that any judoist or amateur wrestler who wants to be successful at sambo must increase his fitness level by at least 50%. Then, he should increase his pain tolerance by 100%. It is my goal to provide a text that can be used by anyone who wants to put on a red jacket or a blue jacket and test his or her soul in the rugged sport of sambo.

Steve Scott

FOREWORD

There are not many books in circulation that focus on the sport of sombo. The skills presented in this book are based on real-world experience. These moves have been used on all levels of competition. I am glad Steve Scott put on paper what he has been teaching for many years.

The sport of sombo is physically demanding. It is as tough as Olympic style wrestling and as skillful as judo or jujitsu. A skilled sombo athlete is truly dangerous from about any position on the mat, whether it be standing or on the ground. This book focuses in on the grappling aspect of sombo, and it does so in a systematic and realistic way.

The sombo skills presented in this book can be applied to mixed martial arts, judo and jujitsu. The philosophy that form follows function is the reason it is such an effective style of grappling. Sombo is adaptable to almost any form of personal combat.

The author, Steve Scott, is a skilled coach and technician in judo, sombo, jujitsu and mixed martial arts. The techniques taught in this book are a compilation of forty years of training, competing and coaching around the world. Steve has been my judo and sombo coach for many years and I was pleased to have some input in this book. I believe it will be something that you can refer to again and again as a source of practical, and effective, technical information.

Chris Heckadon
FIAS World Sombo Champion
World Cup Silver Medalist
National AAU Champion

WHAT IS SAMBO?

ITS HISTORY AND TRADITION

Years ago, a writer for the local newspaper in Kansas City was covering a sambo tournament I promoted. This was a national event and we had a good many elite sambo wrestlers in town for the tournament. Naturally, there was a lot of serious action going on and I guess this reporter was expecting something different. When his brief story on the tournament came out in the next day's paper, he wrote in his opening sentence; "Sambo is not for the faint of heart." He was right.

Sambo isn't for the faint of heart. It's a rugged style of grappling that seems to attract the heartiest of souls. Simply put, it's jacket wrestling from Russia, but in fact, it's a whole lot more.

Sambo, coming out of the dark days of Stalin's regime in the old Soviet Union, has made a lasting impact on the world of sport and self-defense. Sambo has altered how many people in judo, jujitsu, mixed martial arts and other fighting sports have looked at these martial arts. I know that my first sport, judo, has been changed forever (and for the better in my opinion) because of sambo's influences.

When Soviet athletes appeared on the international scene in the late 1950s and early 1960s, they changed the way sport was done. Any sport. Their training methods were the best in the world. The Soviet Union was, among other things, a sports machine that cranked out world-class athletes every year...seemingly getting better every year until the wall came crumbling down...both literally and figuratively.

The sambo wrestlers of the Soviet Union entered onto the world stage of judo in the early 1960s. Sambo men, wearing judo suits, entered the European Judo Championships in 1962 and won five medals. This was the world's first look at this strange form of wrestling and it certainly changed the way everyone did any form of wrestling or grappling ever since those men walked onto that judo mat.

Sambo is an international sport practiced in many countries. While it's true that athletes from nations once controlled by the old Soviet empire continue to dominate the sport, countries such as the United States, Japan, Great Britain, France, Spain, Venezuela and Italy have strong teams.

15

These Soviet sambo wrestlers didn't approach judo the way the Japanese did. The sambo men didn't train to perfect a technique, as was the accepted Japanese (and world) view of judo. Instead, these sambo men trained to become proficient with techniques in a variety of situations. Emphasizing utility over aesthetics, they molded the technique to work for them and had no qualms about changing a move to make it work for their own body type or weight class. And while the judo men favored throwing, the sambo men worked hard to secure submissions. These early sambo men made everyone in judo realize that making an opponent tap out was as good as throwing him.

Sambo is a Russian acronym which means "self-defense without weapons (SAMo-zashchita Bez Oruzhiya) and was developed as a result of the Soviet government's effort to have a system of practical, personal combat for its soldiers. It's easy to say that sambo is "Russian judo" or "Russian jujitsu" and while that description gives a general picture of what it is, it's like calling judo "Japanese wrestling."

Sambo is an exciting sport that is an extreme physical challenge to anyone who participates in it.

Sambo is a wide-open style of grappling featuring throws, takedowns, holds, arm-locks and leglocks. The rules of the sport have changed since the sport's inception before World War II, but not very much.

At the left is a spectacular throw that demonstrates the variety of skills seen in the sport. While this book features the groundfighting skills of sambo, throwing techniques are a very large part of the sport.

Sambo is also spelled "sombo" which is the spelling first used, to my knowledge, in the early 1980s here in the United States. The "o" spelling was used to have Americans use the "ah" sound rather than the "aa" sound in the name. The phonetic spelling helped and most Americans now pronounce the name of the sport correctly. I remember back in the 1970s when I became involved in sambo, most people pronounced it wrong. Actually, sambo was not officially called "sambo" until after World War II. From what I've heard and read, it was simply called "wrestling" and may have gone by other names as well. It was Anatoli Kharlempiev who popular-ized the name "sambo" for this system of self-defense.

It was the Soviet leader Lenin who decreed that the Soviet military needed a hand-to-hand combat method in the early 1920s, so a man named Vasili Oshchepkov, along with others, started work on the development of a new fighting system. Oshchepkov had lived in Japan as a young man and earned a 2nd degree black belt in judo in 1917, making him one of the first non-Japanese to earn a black belt in the newly-developed style of jujutsu called Kodokan Judo. Oshchepkov and his associates traveled the Soviet Union in an effort to study and categorize the various ethnic wrestling and fighting sports and incorporate them into a workable system of hand-to-hand combat. By the 1930s, sambo was being practiced by Soviet troops and sambo clubs were springing up in various cities. By 1939, sambo was being contested on the national level in the Soviet Union and organized as a sport.

What Oschepkov did, was to evaluate the judo he learned in Japan, combine it with what he and his team of assistants discovered in the various Soviet republic wrestling styles (each region pretty much had their own local folk style of grappling, fighting or wrestling and Oschepkov toured the country to study them) and formulate the beginnings of sambo.

The author refereeing a match at the first National AAU Youth Sambo Championships. Traditionally, sambo has attracted athletes from judo and wrestling in the United States, but the Russians have used sambo as their primary approach to wrestling for many years.

The philosophy of using anything that works and is allowed by the rules has given sambo its unique appearance. Anyone who wrestles or does judo can quickly identify someone trained in sambo.

There are two basic versions of sambo. One emphasizing self-defense and the other, covered in the pages of this book, is about sport sambo.

My interest has always been on the sport side of sambo, but I have found that the self-defense techniques used in sambo are efficient, to-the-point and applicable in any situation. While there is much to be learned from the self-defense aspect of sambo, this book will present the sport approach and look at some of the skills that make sambo unique in the world of wrestling and grappling. One book can't possibly do justice to this fascinating sport, so I will present some of the skills that have worked for my athletes and me through our years of involvement in sambo.

Technically, sambo is primarily a throwing and submission sport. I say this because the focus of action is mostly with getting an opponent to the mat and making him submit from a joint lock. The matwork or groundfighting that takes place in sambo all has the ultimate goal of making the opponent submit. Pins or holds are seen as a way of controlling or containing an opponent on the mat until you are able to secure a submission technique. This is unique in a non-Japanese style of grappling and shows that the technical and philosophical roots of sambo are forever linked to the Japanese judo that Vasili Oshchepekov studied as a young man. Presently, the rules of sambo allow for throws, takedowns, holds, elbow submissions and leg submissions. Choking an opponent is not permitted in the sport of sambo, but the self-defense version of sambo allows for pretty much anything that works. I was always fascinated by sambo's attitude of accepting anything that works and the philosophy of molding the technique to make it work for the person doing it.

Sambo was the primary wrestling style in the Soviet Union and the other styles of international wrestling and judo were secondary to their native sport of sambo. This is why sambo so greatly influenced the way the Soviets did judo, freestyle wrestling and Greco-Roman wrestling for many years and why sambo has made such a lasting impression on anyone who participates in wrestling or grappling today. Sambo wrestlers who participate in the many mixed martial arts events popular today prove that sambo places emphasis on both skill and fighting ability. Again, as said in the opening paragraph, sambo isn't for the faint of heart.

Sambo is practiced by both men and women, using the same rules. Using the jacket to manipulate an opponent is an important skill in sambo, both in standing situations and while wrestling on the mat.

The photo at left shows the early seconds of a match at the World Championships with both athletes attempting to control the other and gaining the advantage by means of a dominant grip on the jacket.

Sambo in the United States has been, and continues to be for the most part, technically as good as anywhere else outside of the old Soviet Union. The Russians are still the masters of this sport, but athletes from other countries have made indelible marks on the history of sambo as well. The first American to win a gold medal in the World Sambo Championships was Greg Gibson in 1981. Gibson, a superb and gifted wrestler representing the United States Marine Corps, went on to win the silver medal in Greco-roman wrestling in the 1984 Olympics. The sport of sambo readily accepted women as equals and female athletes from the United States have proven themselves many times on international sambo mats. My wife, Becky Scott, was the first American woman to win a gold medal at the World

Sambo Championships in 1983. Actually, she happened to win her championship match before some of her team-mates did at that same tournament, including her own sister, Jan Trussell, as well as her good friend Grace Jividen.

Sambo's use of leg submissions have been studied by athletes and coaches in many grappling and fighting sports. Most of the leg submissions seen today in mixed martial arts contests come directly from sambo.

Sambo became a world sport when the first World Sambo Championships were held in 1973 in Tehran, Iran. The first National AAU (Amateur Athletic Union) Sambo Championships for men were held in 1975 in Arizona and in 1980 in Kansas City, Missouri for women. Sambo was considered a third discipline of amateur wrestling (along with freestyle and Greco-Roman) by FILA, the international governing body for wrestling, from 1968 through 1984. In 1984, FILA dropped sambo from its program and the International Amateur Sambo Federation (FIAS) was organized. In 1985, the United States Sombo Association was formed, and served as the technical body working with the Amateur Athletic Union in promoting the sport of sambo in the United States.

Sambo was a recognized sport in the 1983 Pan American Games in Caracas, Venezuela. The United States was well-represented by both a full men's team and a full women's team and was very successful. The U.S. women's team won the team championship.

When sambo wasn't selected as a demonstration sport in the 1980 Moscow Olympics or the 1984 Los Angeles Olympics, the sport began to decline in popularity. However, there are still many people training in sambo today, especially in the countries that once comprised the old Soviet Union. Sambo is seeing some newfound popularity as the result of sambo men who have done well in the various mixed martial arts events held all over the world in recent years. Much like its initial rise in popularity back in the 1960s when the Soviet sambo men took the judo world by storm, a younger generation of sambo athletes are winning in the new international sporting event of mixed martial arts.

Sambo, by its very nature, is an eclectic and wide open approach to mat combat. Embracing a philosophy of effectiveness over beauty, it is no wonder that grapplers, fighters and wrestlers all over the world have discovered that sambo is worth learning.

19

Lynn Roethke, Olympic silver medalist in judo, Pan American Games Champion in sambo and World Championship bronze medalist in sambo, once described sambo very well: "It's everything you wanted to do in judo, but weren't allowed to." And you know, Lynn was pretty much right on the money.

SECTION ONE:
The Core Skills of Groundfighting

"Technique is the foundation, not the house."
John Taylor

Sambo is unique because it is such an eclectic style of grappling. But, as with any form of wrestling or grappling, there are fundamental skills that have to be learned and drilled on often and correctly so they are instinctive.

Position, the art of being in the right place and the right time and putting your opponent in the wrong place for him, is extremely important. No matter what style of mat combat you practice, if you don't get into a good position and control your opponent's body and movement, you won't beat him. Before you make him tap out, you have to set him up.

A major goal in groundfighting is to establish a position of control and dominate your opponent. A rule of thumb is to try to get behind your opponent. Another way of saying this is to "get your opponent's back." If you get behind your opponent and establish a strong ride position, he won't be able to see what you are doing. By the same token, never allow your opponent to get behind you.

Also, the body has a lot of handles. Every part of an opponent's body, jacket or belt is a handle for you to use to control him. It doesn't matter what body part you use to control him, whether it be a shoulder, arm, foot or hip. Use whatever handle you need to control and break your opponent down. The jacket and belt are great handles and many sambo techniques use the opponent's jacket or belt.

It's important to be methodical and aggressive in groundfighting. Patience is a virtue in wrestling on the mat. Methodically go from one point of control to the next. Take your time, but do it in a hurry!

Another good point about position is that sometimes, when you are in a bad position, the best thing you can do is to get out of that bad position and into a neutral one. I call these "get out of trouble moves" and they are important to know. If your opponent is in the top position and dominating you, you have to know how to get out of trouble.

Always remember that if you control the position, you control your opponent.

Another core skill in sambo groundfighting is breaking your opponent down from a stable to an unstable position and effectively apply a hold or submission. I call these skills breakdowns. No opponent will willingly let you slap an armlock or leglock on him. You have to break him down and secure the technique.

Some people refer to these skills as turnovers, but I prefer to call them breakdowns as it better describes the wide range of skills used to set an opponent up for a hold or submission technique. You don't always turn him over. You may want him flat on his face. The goal is to take him from a stable position to an unstable (for him) position. The term breakdown also implies a more aggressive approach to groundfighting.

In addition to position, this section will show some breakdowns that have a high ratio of success and can be used by wrestlers of all weight classes. The importance of breakdowns cannot be stressed enough. Get good at them and use them.

A piece of advice I like to tell my athletes is that if you're fighting your opponent on even terms, then you haven't planned out your fight well enough. Do everything you can to control all aspects of the match or fight. An important part of controlling the match is to be in the best position possible as often as possible and do your best to put your opponent in the worst position possible for him.

POSITION

Sambo, or any form of grappling for that matter, is a series of positions that set up other positions only to be countered by another position. Every move you make with your body is a position. How you control these movements and the movements of others determines your success as an athlete. The next few pages show some of the many positions that take place in the sport of sambo. The best advice I can give is that if you control the position, you control your opponent. That's what groundfighting is all about.

Chris Heckadon in a classic "**wrestler's ride**" position. A good rule of thumb is to always try to get behind your opponent and don't allow him to get behind you. This way, you have a higher ratio of success in controlling the situation and in breaking your opponent down so you can gain further control or apply a submission hold. Notice that Chris "has his opponent's back" and can apply an armlock or leglock from this position.

Elbows and Knees Position and Top Standing Position

Steve, the bottom wrestler, is on his **elbows and knees**. Notice that he isn't on his hands and knees. Try never to extend or straighten your arms when in the down position. Keep your arms bent. If you straighten your arms, you are giving your opponent a better chance to quickly apply a straight arm lock. Just as important, by keeping your arms bent, you can react more quickly to any situation that arises. You have more mobility with bent arms.

Also notice the bottom wrestler's feet. He's on the balls of his feet and they are not relaxed. He has more mobility in this position.

The top wrestler, Bill, has his hands on the bottom man with good distribution of weight evenly placed on his feet so he can quickly move to a better position. This position takes place immediately after the top wrestler throws his opponent and the opponent may roll to his elbows and knees getting off his back.

The top wrestler can now further dominate the bottom man by not allowing him to get to his feet, get to his opponent's back to work a submission hold or attempt a breakdown to a hold for time.

Top Ride Position and the Chicken Position

Chris Heckadon is in the top ride position and dominating his opponent who is in the "chicken" position.

Chris had thrown his opponent, who quickly rolled onto his front. Chris immediately got to his opponent's back and took a control position with this ride. Notice that Chris is using his legs to help pin his opponent's lower body to the mat as he starts to look for a handle to secure further control. Chris went on to work a cross body armlock for the submission.

The opponent is in the chicken position because he doesn't know what to do. This is a purely defensive position and not recommended. This is like an ostrich sticking his head in the sand hoping the threat will leave.

Getting Behind Your Opponent to the Standing Ride

This is a ride position that is used in sambo and judo. The idea is to get behind your opponent and quickly dig your feet in. As soon as you get behind your opponent, immediately dig your leg (or legs) in and control his hips. Steve, the top wrestler, will dig his left leg into his opponent's hip and crotch to better control him with his leg. This will then set up a roll into an armlock or Steve can turn around and face to Bill's back and work a near-leg ride knee lock.

Here is a good example of the rodeo ride in judo. The top athlete has his opponent firmly in control. Notice the excellent leg control as well as the hands controlling the upper body using the lapels. It's important not to hook your ankles as this limits your ability to manipulate and control your opponent with your feet.

The Rodeo Ride

The rodeo ride is achieved when the top wrestler has successfully gone behind his opponent and "got his back." Bill, on top, has dug his feet into Steve's hips and crotch and is controlling the lower body well. Bill has underhooked Steve's arms for upper body control.

Bill has rolled Steve off his base and will work to secure a hold or submission technique. This is good leg wrestling. It's important to control the opponent's lower body so he can't get to a strong base or to his feet before you attempt a submission. When you get your opponent's back, you have excellent control of his body and he is vulnerable to a variety of moves, especially submissions.

Becky Scott working behind her opponent and about to dig in with her legs to establish a rodeo ride. Going behind your opponent to a strong position and further controlling her with good leg wrestling is essential in securing a submission hold. Notice that Becky's opponent is in the "chicken" position and completely defensive.

Fighting From The Bottom (The Guard)

If you've just been taken down or thrown, this position is good to know. Many sambo wrestlers with a judo or jujitsu background prefer to fight from this position. But if you do, make sure that you are active and aggressive. Do not lay on your back and wrap your legs around the top wrestler and hook your ankles. This is passive wrestling.

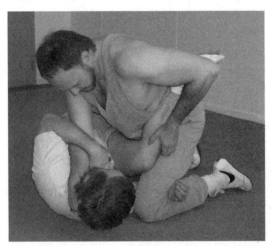

Bill has shrimped to his right and is starting a spinning cross body armlock out of the guard position. This photo shows why this position is a good one. There are many aggressive moves that can be done from here, especially armlocks.

This position is good if you have just escaped from a between legs chest hold and want to counter with an attack of your own.

Rollovers from the Bottom

Another aspect of fighting from the bottom position is knowing how to roll an opponent over and get to the top position. The photo below shows the shrimp and underhook from the bottom and illustrates how being skilled at fighting off your buttocks can get you out of trouble. Sambo requires that you be adaptable in all phases of groundfighting.

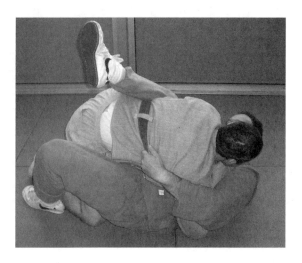

Control Your Opponent's Lower Body

In every aspect of groundfighting, you need to control your opponent's lower body (his hips and legs) before you can work a submission technique. If you don't, he can shuck you off or escape easily. Don't get in too much of a hurry to apply a submission hold until you control his legs and hips.

Leg Press Position

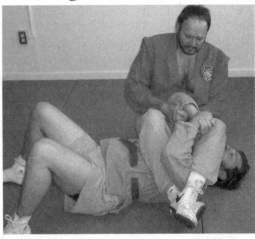

This is a stabilizing position that the top wrestler takes when he rolls his opponent over onto his back. Notice how Steve, the top wrestler, is sitting on his buttocks right by Bill's shoulder and pressing with his legs. The bottom wrestler's shoulder and upper arm are planted in the top wrestler's crotch. Steve controls Bill by squeezing his knees together and hooking his ankles (not always needed).

Steve is pulling in with his feet on Bill's far shoulder, causing it to "accordion." This keeps the bottom wrestler from getting his shoulders square or stable.

A Stable Base

In the above photo, notice that the top wrestler has a stable base with his legs, feet and hips. Your base is like the foundation to a house. If you don't have a balanced and strong base, your grappling skills will be compromised.

Stay Round

In many instances, you will need to be "round" or in the "shrimp" position. Often, when applying an armlock or leglock, you will need to roll your opponent into position to secure the submission. Don't be stiff or too angular in a submission wrestling sport like sambo. In such moves as the gator roll ankle lock or hip roll cross body armlock, you will need to roll your opponent into a more vulnerable position for him. Good flexibility and functional strength are essential to be able to perform effective sambo.

The wrestler above has rolled his opponent in the "gator roll" and applied an ankle lock. Staying round and being able to roll an opponent into a move is important.

Above are two good examples of staying round. The top wrestler is applying a hip roll cross body armlock. Notice that his body is rounded and not flat or angular. His round, rolling movement will help to secure the armlock.

BREAKDOWNS

Knowing how to break an opponent down from a stable to an unstable position is a fundamental skill. Your opponent won't just let you jump on him and secure a hold or submission technique, you have to put him in the position you want and then secure a hold down or make him tap out. There are many ways of breaking an opponent down and what is presented here represents only part of this fascinating phase of grappling. These breakdowns are the some of the ones my athletes have used with great success over the years.

Some people call these moves "turnovers." I prefer to call them breakdowns for two reasons. First, you do more than simply turn an opponent over when you do these moves. You break him down from a stable to an unstable position and sometimes you don't have to turn him over. You may want to "get his back" so you can apply a submission technique from that position. Breakdowns can be done from almost any position, whether it be from a ride position or from fighting off your buttocks. Second, the term "breakdown" implies an aggressive attitude. It's not a passive approach to wrestling. The phrase "turnover" doesn't convey the aggressive attitude you must have to win at groundfighting.

Far Arm-Near Leg Breakdown

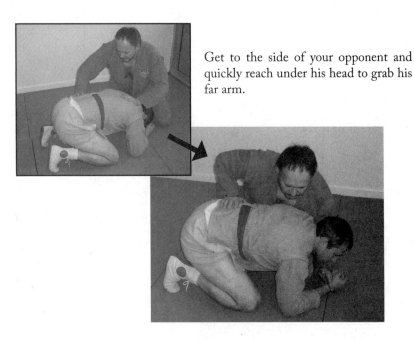

Get to the side of your opponent and quickly reach under his head to grab his far arm.

Don't grab his jacket. Instead, hook his elbow low near the mat with your hand.

Scoop his elbow in toward you. Notice the top wrestler is also placing his chest on the bottom wrestler's near side.

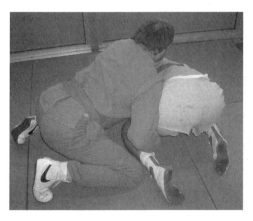

As the top wrestler hooks the bottom wrestler's far elbow, he grabs the near leg at the thigh. Notice that the top wrestler has jammed his shoulder in his opponent's near hip. The top wrestler is also now driving into his opponent with his chest to start the breakdown. The top wrestler is driving off of his toes and his knees are wide providing a solid base.

Steve, the top wrestler, pulls in on his opponent's far elbow and at the same time lifts the near leg and rolls the bottom wrestler over onto his back. Do not pick your opponent up. Instead, roll him over and keep driving into him with your chest.

Steve has rolled his opponent, Shawn, over onto the back. Do not let go of the near leg too soon. The top wrestler should keep the near leg and drive his opponent over and onto his back completely.

The top wrestler must immediately secure a chest hold or other holddown. Be sure to stay low and keep constant contact with you chest as you roll your opponent over. There are many variations of this move, but while this may look simple, it has been used at all levels of sambo, judo and wrestling competition.

Belt and Nelson Breakdown

From the front position as shown, the top wrestler, Steve, positions himself at his opponent's front left shoulder. As he does this, Steve grabs Shawn's belt with his left hand (palm down-this is important). Steve also lays his forearm on Shawn's spine as shown.

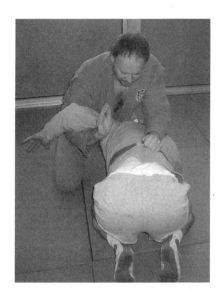

Keeping control with the left hand on the belt and forearm on the spine, Steve now underhooks Shawn's left arm. Notice that the top wrestler's right hand is positioned with fingers pointed to the ceiling and elbow to the mat. Steve scoops Shawn's arm tightly near the shoulder as shown.

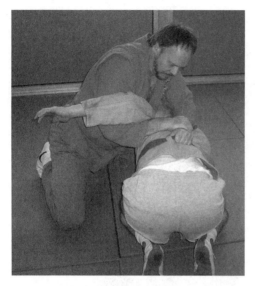

Steve quickly grabs his left wrist with his right hand. Do not grab the belt-grab your own wrist. You have better control of your opponent by grabbing your wrist and not his belt. Remember, the top wrestler's left hand is palm down grabbing the belt.

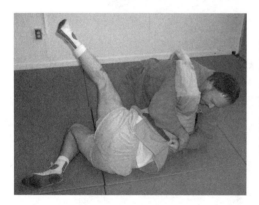

As Steve does this, he moves to his right and under the bottom wrestler's shoulder as shown in the photo. Doing this keeps the bottom wrestler from sitting out or spinning through to escape. Notice Steve is still on his solid base and driving into the move.

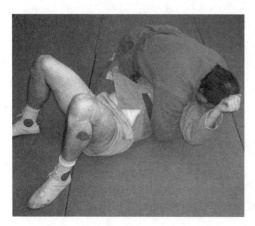

Steve now drives Shawn to the mat, keeping hold of the belt the whole time. Do not let go of the belt. Steve drives hard with his chest and quickly secures Shawn in a chest hold. Steve keeps holding the belt and secures the chest hold.

Belt and Nelson when Opponent is Flat

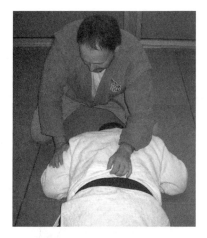

This is a good variation of the belt and nelson when your opponent is laying flat on his front in the chicken position. The top wrestler positions himself at the left shoulder of his opponent as shown.

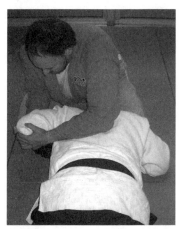

The top wrestler, Steve, quickly lifts Eric's left elbow off the mat with both of his hands. Notice also that Steve has his left elbow wedged into Eric's back giving him leverage and causing some discomfort to his opponent. Steve makes sure he is positioned at the top of Eric's left shoulder as shown in the photo.

Steve gets down and closer to Eric and as he does, he scoops under Eric's left elbow as shown. As he scoops the elbow, Steve draws it toward him.

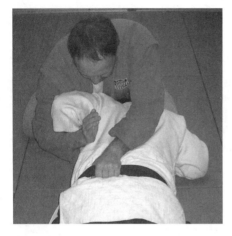

Steve quickly grabs Eric's belt with his left hand (palm down). Steve's forearm is positioned as shown, right along his opponent's spine. As he does this, Steve continues to scoop Eric's left elbow in. There is no room between Steve's chest and Eric's left shoulder as you can see in the photo at left.

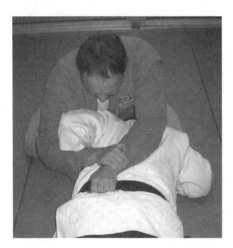

Steve now grabs his left wrist with his right hand all the while, scooping up on Eric's left elbow. The top wrestler also makes a point to start to move to his left.

As in the basic approach to belt and nelson, it is important to grab your own wrist and not both hands on your opponent's belt.

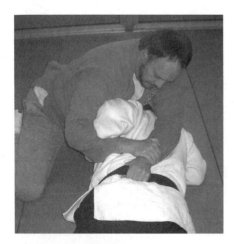

Steve has moved to his right and under Eric's left shoulder. Steve drives hard with his chest on Eric's shoulder as he continues to scoop Eric's left elbow. The top wrestler should drive hard and not expect the bottom wrestler to roll over easily. He doesn't want to go on his back, so drive him over aggressively.

This photo shows the mid-point of the breakdown. Steve, on top, is hugging Eric's left elbow tightly and driving into him with his chest. Do not let go of the belt with your left hand at any time.

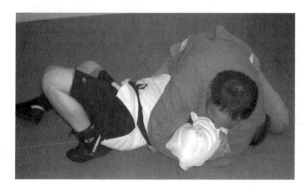

Steve has driven Eric over onto his back and has secured the chest hold. The top wrestler should keep hold of the belt as long as possible to maintain total control of his opponent.

Keylock Breakdown

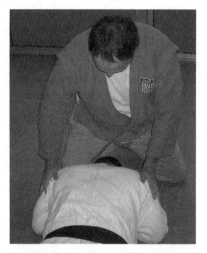

Steve has positioned himself at the top of Eric's head as shown in the photo. Eric is in the chicken position, flat on his front. Often, wrestlers believe they can kill time and stall by laying in this chicken position. Other wrestlers may hide like this for lack of knowing what to do from the bottom position. Like the ostrich sticking his head in the sand, they hope the threat will go away.

Steve, on top, traps Eric's head by driving his right knee directly on Eric's shoulder. Eric's head is now stuck between Steve's legs. As Steve does this, he places his right elbow on Eric's back and scoops under Eric's right elbow with both of his hands as shown.

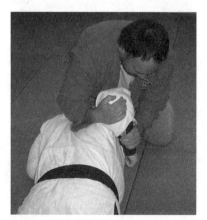

As he continues to pull in and scoop up on Eric's right elbow, Steve now firmly grabs Eric's right wrist. Notice that Steve is low and has pulled Eric's elbow to his chest.

Steve now quickly hooks his right arm through Eric's right arm as shown and will immediately grab his own wrist. Steve has also clamped his legs tightly on Eric's head at this point.

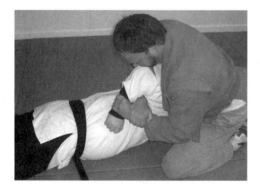

Steve firmly grabs his left wrist with his right hand and secures the keylock. As he does this, the top wrestler starts to move to his left and under the bottom wrestler's chest as shown.

Steve now pulls Eric's elbow to his chest to add more control to the breakdown and to weaken his opponent. The wrestler may have to bring his chest to Eric's elbow, but make every attempt to bring his elbow to the chest.

Steve now moves to his left more and drives hard into Eric as shown.

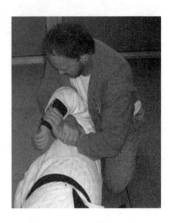

The top wrestler often has to let go of his left hand on the bottom wrestler's wrist at this point and scoop the elbow as shown. Doing this helps tighten the control of the bottom wrestler's trapped right arm to the top wrestler's chest. Steve, the top wrestler, drives hard into Eric forcing him onto his back. Steve then secures a chest hold.

The Sambo Switch

This is a classic "get out of trouble move" and every wrestler should know it. The bottom wrestler, Bill, is on his hands and elbows and Eric is at his top. Bill realizes he is not in the best of positions, so he must do something to get out of trouble.

Bill immediately drives his left shoulder into Eric's left hip and positions his head on Eric's hip. Bill's left ear is firmly wedged onto Eric's left hip at this point. Doing all of this, Bill is now very close to Eric and can hook between Eric's legs and grab the left leg with his left hand.

Bill clasps his hands together and sucks Eric's knee and leg into him as he starts to move to the right. Notice that Bill is on his knees and driving off of his toes. Important: Bill does not reach for Eric's leg with his left arm, as Eric could sit through and secure an armlock. Bill stays tight and compact.

45

Bill continues to wedge his left ear on Eric's hip as he continues to hold Eric's knee and leg with his grasped hands. Bill makes sure to stay on his knees and "turn the corner" by moving quickly to his right and around toward Eric's back side and legs. Bill also drives with his head against Eric's hip.

Important: Do not attempt to sit through if you are the bottom wrestler. Stay on your knees and toes. You have much better position doing it this way rather than trying to sit through. The top wrestler can often hook the bottom wrestler's head as he attempts to sit through.

Bill has now turned the corner and gone behind Eric. Notice that Bill continues to keep his left ear tightly positioned on Eric.

Bill is in the top ride position and has Eric's back. He can now work to secure a stronger position or breakdown. Often, getting out of trouble is the only thing you can do. The sambo switch is one of those moves that may not be fancy, but does the job when you need it.

Front 2-Leg Breakdown

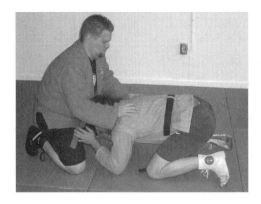

The bottom wrestler, Bill, is on his elbows and knees with his opponent, Eric, at the top. Bill needs to get out of this situation.

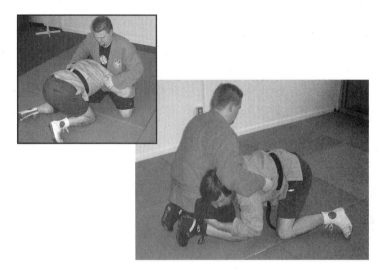

Bill quickly gets his head out of the middle of Eric's legs and positions it on Eric's right hip. As Bill does this, he closes the space between his shoulders and Eric's hips and driving into him as shown.

Bill wedges his right shoulder firmly into Eric's mid-section and plants his right ear on Eric's right hip. Bill is careful to keep his knees wide and drive off his toes. Bill has also grabbed each of Eric's legs just above the knees. Do not grab your hands together. Hook onto the legs just above his knees with each of your hands.

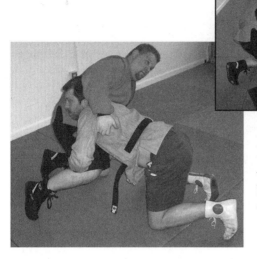

Bill now scoops both of Eric's legs to the left as he drives very hard with his head to the right. This is basically a double leg takedown off the knees.

Bill drives hard to his right and scoops Eric's legs. Notice how Bill has to drive off his feet. Eric will land mostly on his left side.

Bill quickly works up Eric's body and secures a chest hold. At no time during the breakdown did Bill separate his body from Eric. He kept constant contact the whole time.

Sambo Stack

The bottom wrestler is on his face in the chicken position. The situation might have been that the top wrestler just threw his opponent and the opponent turned over onto his front as a defensive move.

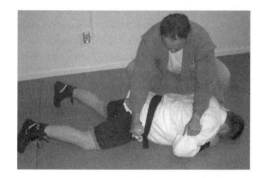

The top wrestler, Steve, positions himself to the side of the bottom wrestler as shown and squats. Do not kneel, be sure to squat with one foot at the opponent's shoulder and the other at his hip. As Steve does this, he reaches across his opponent's body and grabs the jacket sleeve mid-way between the shoulder and elbow with his left hand and just below the belt on the jacket apron with his right hand. Steve's elbows should be close to his opponent's back for added leverage.

In an explosive movement, Steve lunges back and snatches his opponent close to him, dragging him onto his back. The top wrestler must take care not to fall back, but rather spring back from the initial squat.

Steve keeps his grip on both the sleeve and jacket apron of the bottom wrestler. Making sure to plant the bottom wrestler's shoulder and hip to the mat, the top wrestler forcefully drives the bottom wrestler to the mat.

The top wrestler can either immediately secure a cross body armlock (top photo) or a chest hold (bottom photo). The sambo stack is an aggressive breakdown, and even if the first attempt at doing it is unsuccessful, the top wrestler can drag his opponent across the mat and make the breakdown work on the second or even third try.

Soden Roll

The bottom wrestler, Shawn, is on his elbows and knees with Steve over him. This breakdown is especially useful when the top wrestler reaches over the arms of the bottom wrestler to grab the jacket.

Shawn clamps onto Steve's arms as shown and works his head to the side he will roll, in this case, to the left. As he does this, he sits through with his right leg as shown.

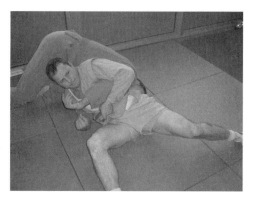

As Shawn sits through, he continues to roll Steve with him. Notice that Shawn has clamped tightly onto both of Steve's arms just above the elbow.

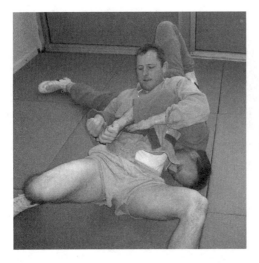

Shawn completes his sit through, rolling Steve completely over onto his back. Shawn maintains tight control of both of Steve's arms.

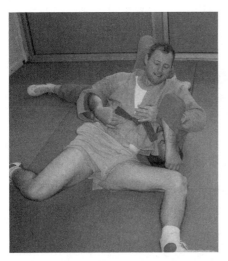

Shawn has rolled Steve over onto his back and makes sure to jam his left hip between Steve's left shoulder and neck. Notice the leg position that gives Shawn a strong base.

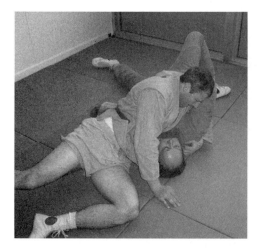

To get the chest to chest contact for the purposes of a sambo hold, Shawn continues to roll onto Steve. Shawn keeps his left arm hooked under Steve's armpit and posts with his left hand on the mat for stability.

Shawn then hooks under Steve's neck with his left arm and hugs him causing chest contact and the hold to be in effect.

Peterson Roll

This breakdown is useful if the top wrestler reaches too far with his arm as shown.

The bottom wrestler hooks the arm of the top wrestler just above the elbow, and as he does this, the bottom wrestler, Shawn, shifts back sticking his buttock out to the right. This positions the top wrestler, to the left side of the bottom wrestler. This position allows for a better rolling action by the bottom wrestler.

Shawn rolls Steve over his back as shown in the photo. Notice that Shawn has drawn Steve in very close and there is no body space between the two wrestlers. Shawn maintains his hook just above Steve's elbow and cinches it in tightly. Shawn does this so Steve won't be able to post his right arm out and stop the rolling motion.

To assist the roll, Shawn has hooked under Steve's near leg (in this case, Steve's right leg). Shawn lifts on the leg to help roll his opponent over his body.

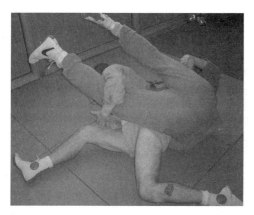

Here is another view of the roll with Shawn hooking Steve's leg. Notice that Shawn's legs are important in making this roll happen. Shawn drives off his feet and sits through if necessary to assist the rolling movement. Additionally, Shawn has turned his hips forcefully and very quickly, which helps in the rolling movement.

Shawn has rolled Steve onto his back, maintaining his hold of Steve's leg.

Shawn now positions his lower body as shown with his buttocks on the mat and feet planted firmly. He does this so he can turn to his left immediately. Shawn firmly keeps his overhook on Steve's right arm all the while.

Shawn now quickly reverses his position and rolls onto Steve as shown. Shawn reaches around Steve's torso and grabs the belt or jacket, or simply hooks the torso at the far hip. Notice Shawn's base with his leg position for stability and strength. Shawn sucks Steve's right arm in tightly to his body which maintains upper body control and causes discomfort.

Shrimp and Underhook from the Bottom

This move is useful if the bottom wrestler has tried a spinning cross body armlock and failed, or if he breaks chest contact with the top wrestler (as shown) and wants to counter with a move of his own.

Steve, on bottom, shrimps to his right, and as he does, hooks under Shawn's left leg. Steve makes sure to get his right ear as close to Shawn's left knee as possible. As Steve does this, he also drives his right leg across Shawn's rib cage.

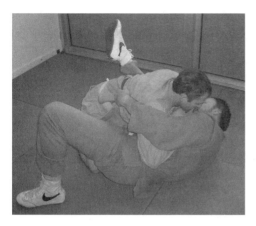

As he does the moves shown in the photo above, Steve also makes sure to reach over Shawn's right arm-across the deltoid-between the elbow and shoulder. Steve grabs Shawn's belt, or if that isn't possible, grabs Shawn's jacket. Steve is careful to clamp down tightly on Shawn's right arm with his left arm, trapping the arm and preventing Shawn from posting with it on the mat.

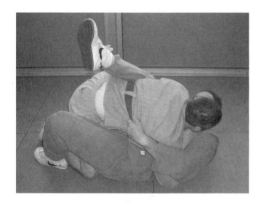

Steve, on the bottom, has now blocked Shawn's right leg with his left leg. Steve is careful to plant his left foot on the mat so he can drive off of it.

Steve forcefully scoops under Shawn's right leg as he pulls on the belt with his left hand. Also notice that Steve's right foot is pointed, giving him more power.

This photo is another view. Notice that Steve is scooping hard with his right hand under Shawn's left knee and he rolls Shawn over.

Steve rolls back over his left shoulder and upper back. Steve drives off of his left foot as he rolls back over his left shoulder. Momentum is important, so be sure to stay as round as possible when rolling back over your shoulder.

As the roll is completed, Steve takes care to continue all the way until he is completely on top of his opponent.

Steve now has rolled Shawn onto his back and continues on with a vertical chest hold.

SECTION TWO:
The Holds of Sambo

"Plant him there until he quits."
Shawn Watson

The primary purpose of holds or hold-downs in sambo is to immobilize your opponent so that you can eventually work a submission technique on him. Unlike other amateur styles of wrestling, the goal is not to pin your opponent's shoulders to the mat. In sambo, the goal is to force him to submit with a joint hold.

In a sambo match, under the current rules, a wrestler can accumulate four points for hold-downs. It can come from one 20-second hold or from two 10-second holds. So then, it's not possible to defeat an opponent using a hold-down as in the sport of judo where holding an opponent down for 25 seconds results in a victory.

The rules of sport sambo are specific in that once a wrestler has accumulated the twenty seconds in his hold, he must immediately attempt to secure a submission technique. Simply letting an opponent up after a hold is considered passive wrestling, so it is important for a sambo wrestler to learn how to make the transition from a hold-down to a submission technique as quickly and as effectively as possible. Another feature of sambo hold-downs is that there must be chest to chest contact, or at least torso to torso contact. The reasoning behind this is to insure complete control over the opponent. Also, unlike judo, a sambo wrestler doesn't have to be free of his opponent's legs to secure a hold. If the top wrestler has secured a holddown and the bottom wrestler manages to scissor the legs of the top man, the hold is still in effect. Chest contact must be broken to nullify the hold and a good part of the referee's job is to watch for any break in the chest or torso contact between the two wrestlers.

It's always a good idea to follow through to the mat after a throw or takedown with a submission technique, and if that's not possible, follow through with a hold-down to immobilize your opponent and give yourself time to work a submission technique.

A nice "chain" as my friend Jim Schneweis calls it, is to throw your opponent and pick up points for that. Immediately follow through with a hold and pick up points for that, then attempt to secure a submission technique and finish the match. This throw-hold-submission chain is a good strategy.

Another feature of sambo that is different from other styles of wrestling is that no points are awarded for escapes or reversals. The idea in sambo is score points only for offensive action. If you manage to escape or reverse the situation, good for you, but you don't get any credit for it other than avoiding defeat.

The holds presented in this section represent the most often-used holding techniques in sambo. Most sambo wrestlers have done these hold-downs, but I'm presenting them here as I teach them. Don't hesitate to alter any of the holds shown to fit your particular needs. The idea is to immobilize your opponent, giving yourself time and increasingly more control of your opponent's body in order to secure a submission technique. Shawn Watson's advice is sound. Plant him there until he quits.

Be sure to refer to the Section One (on the core skills) to study some breakdowns that set up these holds. You'll never face an opponent who will willingly allow you to hold him down or make him tap out, so it's important to learn the breakdowns in Section One and link them with the holds shown in this section.

Between Legs Chest Hold

This is a common hold-down in sambo. In this photo, Warren Frank is keeping excellent chest-to-chest contact with his opponent and looking to the side of the mat to see when 20 seconds is up so he can continue on into a submission technique.

Basically, the top wrestler gets between his opponent's legs, makes and maintains chest and torso contact and rides him until the time elapses earning up to 4 points for a 20-second hold. He then immediately works to secure an armlock or leglock.

Steve, the top wrestler, has grabbed Bill at each arm just above the elbow. Another good hold is to grab under the arms to keep tight control. The top wrestler wants to "ride" the bottom to keep him under control and keep him parked there to get maximum points and then work for a submission technique.

Chest-to-Chest Contact Broken

The hold time stops when the bottom wrestler manages to break the chest (or torso) contact between the two bodies. This is the most often used "escape" for this hold-down. When this takes place, both wrestlers will attempt to reposition themselves to regain control or secure a submission. The top wrestler wants to keep contact so he can get 4 points for the hold-down.

Chest Hold

This is a real workhorse in sambo as hold-downs go, an extremely strong hold that is difficult to break. Basically, the top wrestler hugs his opponent and rides him as necessary to keep chest contact and the bottom man on his back.

Notice that Chris, on top, has his knees wide and hips low with his feet close to each other. He has formed a solid base with his lower body and keeps his left knee jammed under his opponent's near shoulder. Chris has positioned his left arm under Bob's neck and attempts to keep him from bridging by jamming his left shoulder in Bob's left jaw and keeping his left elbow on the mat as a base. Chris has hooked under Bob's far arm and grabbed his hands together in a "square" lock.

Chris keeps as much pressure on as possible by squeezing and continually shifting his weight to make sure he stays on top and in control. Also notice Bob's right arm (the one hooked between Chris' armpit and hip. Chris has scooped under Bob's head and neck and jammed his knee under Bob's near shoulder so that Bob's near arm is useless. If Bob could get his arm in and push against Chris' hip or body, he might be able to start his escape.

The chest hold is a useful and popular hold-down in sambo and the hold that I have coached my athletes in as the core hold-down to use. This hold is very strong in keeping your opponent under control and affording excellent chest-to-chest contact throughout the entire hold. It's also a good position to initiate a submission hold, especially bent-arm locks.

The top wrestler shouldn't hesitate to change leg positions to maintain control. Chris can flatten out and place his hips on the mat as shown. This leg position provides a strong base.

Chris, on top, has now shifted his leg and hip position to keep his opponent on the mat. You may have to shift your leg and hips positions during the course of a hold-down in a competitive situation. Be prepared to do what is necessary to maintain chest contact and control of your opponent.

Remember, this isn't a "pin" as in freestyle wrestling where you have to pin your opponent's shoulders to the mat. This is more of a "ride" in that the top wrestler must maintain control over his opponent for 20 seconds.

Here is another example of how the top wrestler hugs his opponent. Steve, on top, has hooked under Bill's left armpit and has his chin jammed in Bill's shoulder. It is important for the top wrestler to not put too much of his weight forward or high into his chest. The top wrestler should have his weight distributed evenly with his hips very low to the mat and much of his weight actually in his hips. This gives the wrestler doing the hold better weight distribution and keeps the bottom wrestler from escaping.

Upper Chest Hold

Kenney Brink has followed through from a throw with this upper chest hold-down. This is a strong way to hold your opponent to the mat and keep chest-to-chest contact. In this hold, Kenney's legs are spread wide and form a solid base.

Notice his hips are fairly low and his toes digging into the mat to provide leverage. Kenney has scooped under his opponent's arms and is grabbing the belt (a great handle).

Above, Shawn is holding Steve with the basic application of the upper chest hold. Shawn's knees are wide and his hips are low. He has scooped under Steve's arms and shoulders and is holding firmly onto his belt. As Steve moves to escape, Shawn will "ride" him, maintaining control.

The top wrestler above, Bill, is holding Eric with a variation of the upper chest hold. Notice that Bill's hips are low and knees are wide to provide a stable base and he is positioned over Eric's right shoulder and chest area. From this position, Bill can quickly work to secure a cross body armlock or other submission hold.

Vertical Chest Hold

The vertical chest hold is a good position to work submissions from and is useful in this regard. Often, a wrestler will have a chest hold or side chest hold, move to this vertical chest hold and then attempt to secure a bent arm lock.

Vertical Chest Hold with Grapevine

A good way to keep the bottom wrestler from getting away is to grapevine his legs as shown. Notice how the top wrestler has locked the bottom wrestler's shoulder, head and arm for good upper body control as well.

Side Chest Hold

Notice that Steve, on top, has scooped his left arm under Eric's neck which prevents Eric from bridging which would weaken the hold. Steve has reached through Eric's legs and is holding onto the jacket or belt.

Shawn has extended his legs to a wide base. His hips are low on the mat and he has dug his toes in the mat as well. Do not hesitate to change your base as necessary to maintain control of your opponent.

Head and Arm Hold

A popular hold and a good follow up hold from a throw or take-down. In the photo above, the top wrestler has scored his four points and is attempting to secure a straight armlock.

The key feature in this hold is for the top wrestler to position his right hip (in the photo at right) deeply into the bottom wrestler's armpit. The top wrestler then pulls on the bottom man's right arm and wraps it around his own body as shown. Shawn, the top wrestler, has a strong base with his legs. The back leg (left leg in the photo) is positioned with the knee on the mat as shown. The right leg is extended forward as shown. This provides a very strong and stable base for this hold. Shawn has hooked under Steve's head to prevent Steve from bridging. Shawn pulls Steve into him as he "rides" him.

Shoulder Trap Hold

A variation of the head and arm hold is the shoulder trap hold. This hold has the same leg and hip position but notice that the top wrestler has hooked under the bottom wrestler's neck and has shoved his arm across the face. The top wrestler squeezes hard, trapping the shoulder, arm and neck of the bottom wrestler together. The top wrestler can lean back a bit to cause discomfort in the bottom man's chest and ribs.

SECTION THREE:
Arm Submissions

"If you make your opponent give up, he'll never forgive you and he'll never forget you."
Steve Scott

Arm submissions, or armlocks, are an integral part of sambo. As I have mentioned elsewhere in this book, sambo is mostly a throwing and submission style of grappling. The goal isn't to pin your opponent, but rather to force him to submit to a joint lock.

Historically, it was the Soviet sambo wrestlers who burst onto the international judo scene in the 1960s and showed that armlocks, especially the cross body armlock, were just as effective as throwing an opponent. Traditionally, judo emphasized throwing techniques over submission techniques as the primary method of winning a match. However, this opinion changed when the sambo wrestlers continually proved that making an opponent tap was as valid as slamming him to the mat. It was this introduction the world had to sambo that changed how every form of grappling on the planet approached armlocks. The Soviet sambo wrestlers were the innovators who changed the world of grappling forever.

The goal of sambo armlocks is to attack the elbow joint, but often the whole arm and shoulder are affected as well. When cranking on an opponent's arm, he will not only feel it in his elbow, he will feel the biceps tendon and muscle stretch and feel great discomfort in his triceps and shoulder as well. The important thing to remember about sambo submissions, for both armlocks and leglocks, is not to twist the joint being attacked. Often, this twisting motion gets out of control and serious injury can take place. Keep the submission within the rules, and you can better (and more safely) control the whole range of the submission technique.

Always, and I mean, always, follow through to the mat with a submission technique after throwing opponent or taking him down. While the rules of sambo allow for a "total victory" from a throw by remaining in an upright and stable position after a throw, it is rare for this to happen. I have always believed that following through to the ground with a submission technique is an "insurance policy." Make sure your opponent is defeated, and making him tap out is a sure sign that he has been defeated.

I have often told my athletes "If you make your opponent give up, he will never forgive you or never forget you." You will have a psychological edge over him the next time you fight him and other people will see that you have the ability to make people submit. Any competitive edge (that's legal) is a plus and could help you win matches.

The core skills presented here should be practiced and become instinctive behavior. Theses skills work and doing them ensures you that your armlocks will be performed with better skill and confidence. These are the "little things" that really aren't so little. They are fundamental, key elements of every successful armlock. These core skills are the glue that hold everything together. Know and apply these skills every time you do armlocks.

CORE SKILLS OF ARMLOCKS

More than the elbow is attacked in armlocks. If you do an armlock right, your opponent will feel it in his biceps, triceps and shoulder as well as in the elbow. Sambo rules don't allow for a twisting motion, so make sure that you straighten or bend the arm rather than twist it.

Leg Press Position

This is a stabilizing position that the top wrestler takes when he rolls his opponent over onto his back. Notice how Steve, the top wrestler, is sitting on his buttocks right by Bill's shoulder and pressing with his legs. The bottom wrestler's shoulder and upper arm are planted in the top wrestler's crotch. Steve controls Bill by squeezing his knees together and hooking his ankles (not always needed). Steve is pulling in with his feet on Bill's far shoulder, causing it to "accordion." This keeps the bottom wrestler from getting his shoulders square or stable.

Knees Up

If you're the bottom wrestler, don't lay flat. Keep your knees up so you can bridge and avoid losing valuable time working your escape.

Sit Up on Buttocks and Hips Close to Opponent's Near Shoulder

After rolling your opponent onto his back, it's important for the top wrestler to sit in an upright position before rolling back to apply pressure as seen at left. By doing this, the top wrestler can scoot his buttocks in even closer to close the gap between his hips and buttocks and the bottom wrestler's near shoulder. By closing this gap, the top wrestler can apply more pressure and have more leverage as well. Warren Frank has just thrown his opponent and followed through with the armlock. He is about to lever the arm free to secure the submission.

Head Up

By keeping your head up, you have better leverage and can see what you (and your opponent) are doing. Jan Trussell has turned her opponent over and is starting to straighten out her arm. Jan's head is up giving her leverage and a good view of the action.

Arch Your Hips

You create more pressure on your opponent's elbow when you arch your hips as you pull on his arm.

Grab His Arm Like a Ball Bat and Pull His Fist to Your Chin

Grab your opponent's wrist like you would a baseball bat and pull it forcefully to your chin. Make sure your head is up off the mat. Don't worry where his little finger or thumb points as some people do. If you grab his arm like a ball bat and stretch it to your chin, you will have his arm in the right position.

Squeeze Your Knees Together

Here's another view of the cross body armlock and squeezing the knees together. Whether it be sambo, judo, jujitsu or mixed martial arts, these fundamentals are important. The photos at left and above show how pinning your opponent's arm by pinching or squeezing your knees together limits his movement greatly.

Control Opponent's Head

Notice how Bill, the top wrestler, has his left leg hooked over his opponent's head and is controlling it. Bill draws his left foot in close to Steve's head and plants his heel firmly in Steve's neck. All the while, he is pressing down hard with his leg on Steve's head to pin it to the mat.

Keep Wrist Off the Mat and Draw His Arm to Your Body

In bent armlocks, keep your opponent's wrist from resting on the mat and draw his arm to your body as you lever his arm. This gives you much more leverage. Don't twist his arm. Keep his arm off the mat and lever it forcefully.

A Word On Submitting

Nobody likes to lose. But nobody likes to have an arm or leg broken either! Sometimes you may be forced to submit. Rather than having your arm broken, make sure you tap twice or yell out. The rules of sambo say that if you tap or make an audible sound, that is a sign of submission. Even if you yell or grunt, it's still audible and the referee will take it to mean that you surrender. This is done so that if you are unable to tap with your hands or feet, you can signal defeat verbally. It's for the safety of the wrestlers and a good rule.

If you tap, it is best to tap your opponent's body forcefully enough for him to feel you tapping, and as an added precaution, yell out "I give up" or "I quit" at the same time. Don't just tap the mat and assume the referee or your opponent know it's you giving up. If you can't tap with your hands, tap the mat with one or both feet. If you are the wrestler applying the submission hold, always, I repeat, always release pressure when the opponent taps (especially in practice) and when the referee signals your victory or blows his whistle. When your opponent taps or yells out, he means it!

If you've been caught in a good submission hold and can't escape, tap out or yell out. Live to fight another round in the tournament or another match another day.

A bruised ego heals much more quickly than a broken arm.

Back Roll Cross Body Armlock

While this is the basic application of this armlock, it is used again and again by every level of sambo wrestler. I remember when Warren Frank used this armlock twice at the World Championships forcing his opponents to tap out each time. This is an excellent follow through after a throw or takedown and this armlock has a high ratio of success.

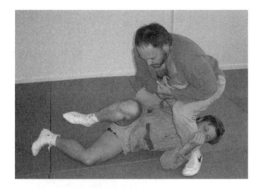

The top wrestler, Steve, has jammed his right leg firmly into Bill's back (the bottom wrestler). Steve's right shin is firmly in Bill's back and ribs. Steve has stepped over Bill's head and is in a squatting position. Steve must squat and stay low so he can more easily roll back.

Notice that Steve has grabbed Bill's arm like a ball bat and trapped is securely to his chest. Steve's left heel is jammed deep into Bill's neck. As Steve starts to roll back, he makes sure to squeeze his knees together to trap Bill's arm. Notice that Steve's back is rounded which allows him to roll back better.

Steve has rolled onto his back and as he did, he pulled Bill's arm tightly into his crotch. Steve is pulling Bill's fist to his chin. His right shin is jammed tightly into Bill's ribs and back and Steve's left leg is hooked over Bill's head for control. Notice the angle from which Steve is applying the armlock. The angle is slightly up and over Bill's shoulder and not square. This angle weakens Bill and adds pressure to the shoulder and stretches the biceps as well.

75

Spin and Stretch to Cross Body Armlock

Here is a good application of this armlock that can be used both as a drill in practice and in competition. I use this as a drill to simulate a throw and a quick follow through to securing the armlock. Rather than take a lot of hard falls every practice, use this drill to reinforce following every throw with a submission. In drilling, I have each wrestler do three full repetitions without resistance, then his partner does his three. I have them do these in sets of three for at least 3 or 4 minutes and each athlete should get at least 30 or 40 repetitions of this move in that period of time. Remember, this is a drill to reinforce this skill and this is why the bottom wrestler does not offer any resistance.

As a takedown, this is very effective. Use this to throw or take your opponent down in situations where he is on his knees. As he tries to get to his feet, use the spin and stretch to throw him for points and then follow through with the armlock, or even with a leglock. My wife, Becky, used this in both sambo and judo with excellent results.

The bottom wrestler is on both knees and attempting to get to his feet. The top wrestler had gripped between the bottom man's shoulder blades on the jacket with his right hand and the jacket at the elbow with his left. If necessary, the top wrestler can drag the bottom wrestler around to keep him in this down position.

The photo at left shows how the top wrestler, Steve, has gripped with his right hand. Do not grip at the collar. Gripping the jacket between your opponent's shoulder blades gives very good control.

Steve steps across Bill's knees and plants his right heel at the side of Bill's right knee. Go to the side, as shown, and not directly forward. Doing this gives the top wrestler better leverage and the chance to spin his opponent to the mat. You don't have to lift him, just spin him to the mat.

Steve is now spinning Bill to the mat. This isn't a throw, but rather a takedown. Steve is controlling Bill firmly with his grip on both the elbow and between the shoulder blades.

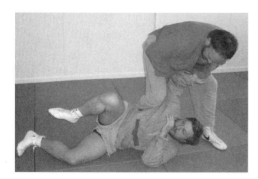

The spin is complete and Steve has now jammed his right shin firmly into the back of Bill's ribs. Notice how Steve has turned into the move to make sure that Bill is firmly on the mat.

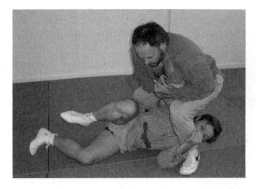

Steve steps over Bill's head as he immediately squats. Notice how Steve has trapped Bill's arm to his chest as he slightly bends over Bill. (Actually squat or sit on the bottom wrestler's head and neck.) Steve pinches Bill's arm tightly with his knees as he rolls back onto his buttocks, then back.

Steve rolls onto his back as he drags Bill's arm with him. Doing this causes the bottom wrestler's arm to stretch causing as much discomfort in the biceps and shoulders as in the elbow. Notice how Steve continues to squeeze his knees together trapping Bill's arm.

Hip Roll Cross Body Armlock

This is an often-used and effective application of this armlock. It can be used by all weight classes with a high ratio of success. This is one of my personal favorites. If you were to have to learn only one way of getting into the cross body armlock, I would recommend this one.

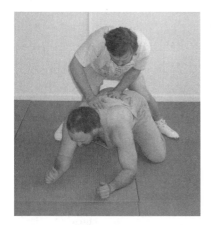

The top wrestler has gone behind the bottom man in a standing ride and keeps control by pushing with his hands.

Bill, on top, has hooked his left leg in Steve's far side. Notice that Bill is not directly to Steve's side. Bill is keeping his weight centered above Steve's hips and low back and is controlling the far hip by jamming his left leg in.

Bill controls the far arm, in this case at the wrist, and has hooked his left leg in deep to Steve's crotch for more control. Bill keeps his weight centered over Steve's body and does not lean too far out over the bottom wrestler.

Bill has now posted his hand, but only momentarily. Bill has started to put more weight into the direction of the roll at this point.

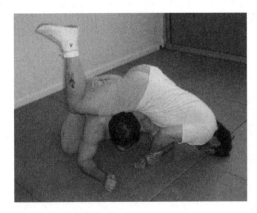

The photo at left shows Bill posting on his head to provide a stable base for himself. Bill is fully committed to the roll and begins to move his right leg over Steve's body (eventually to hook Steve's head). Bill is starting to roll to his own left (in the direction of his hip). Notice that Bill has also trapped Steve's left arm and is pulling it to his chest.

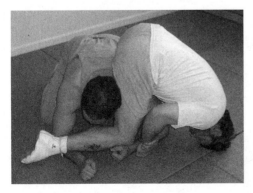

Bill has posted on his head and quickly positions his right leg over Steve's head and neck. Bill constantly pulls Steve's arm to his chest. Notice how Bill is pointing his right toe which gives his leg more power for the hooking action to follow.

Bill rolls over his left shoulder and hooks Steve's head forcefully as shown. Bill makes sure to keep his toe pointed giving his right leg more power. Bill stays round and is in a tight ball as he rolls. He also keeps Steve's arm trapped firmly to his chest as he rolls.

Notice that Bill is tightly in a ball and rolling Steve, forcefully hooking Steve's head with the right leg. Bill's left leg is jammed in Steve's torso and is also hooking, giving the top wrestler further control of the entire body. Bill keeps that arm firmly trapped to his chest.

Bill finishes the roll by coming up onto his buttocks, making sure to keep his hips tight against the near shoulder of the bottom wrestler. Bill keeps his right leg hooked firmly over Steve's head and neck. Notice that Bill is in complete control of the situation. Do not be in a big hurry to flatten out. Get to this position, then roll back.

Another view of the position shown in the previous photo. Also notice how Bill is hooking under Steve's far shoulder. This is a strong leg press position and doing this "accordions" the bottom wrestler's shoulders weakening them.

Also notice that Bill's hips and buttock are extremely close to the bottom wrestler's near shoulder.

Bill completes the arm lock by rolling back and pulling Steve's arm as he does. Bill can arch his hips and add more pressure to the elbow as he pulls on the arm.

Spinning Cross Body Armlock

Before I discuss this armlock, it is important to mention that if a wrestler drops to his butt from a standing position without attempting to work a scoring move such as a throw or takedown, it is considered passivity. This application of the cross body armlock is very effective when the bottom wrestler has found himself, for whatever reason, on his buttocks, back or hips. This spinning application works well for the bottom wrestler who has just broken chest contact with the opponent to escape from a hold-down. Immediately after breaking chest contact, go for this armlock.

Bill, on bottom, has broken chest contact with Steve. Now is a good time for Bill to go for the spinning cross body armlock.

The bottom wrestler, Bill, has trapped Steve's right arm and at the same time, scoots his buttocks in very close to Steve's knees as shown in the photo.

Here is another photo of the previous action. The bottom wrestler should take care to trap his opponent's arm and keep it close to his chest.

Bill has turned his body into a tight ball and shrimps to his right side trying to place his right ear as close to Steve's left knee as possible. At the same time, Bill hooks under Steve's left knee (with his palm facing him) and draws himself even tighter to Steve's knee. Bill also positions his right leg against Steve's rib cage, making sure to point his toes for extra power.

Bill hooks his left leg over Steve's head and neck making sure to point his toes to gain as much hooking power as he can. As he does this, Bill starts to lift with his right arm which is hooking under Steve's leg. Bill drives hard against Steve's neck and head with his left leg and hard against Steve's ribs with his right leg.

Bill has rolled Steve onto his back and immediately scoots his buttocks in as tightly as possible against Steve's near shoulder. It is important for Bill to actually roll up onto his buttocks. By rolling up, the attacking wrestler continues the momentum of the roll and places his hips close to his opponent's near shoulder. Bill continues to hug Steve's right arm in preparation to secure the armlock.

Bill now has completed the roll and has controlled Steve's head with his left leg and Steve's torso with his right leg. Bill hugs Steve's arm close to his chest as he prepares to roll back to secure the armlock. Hugging the arm to the chest helps free the arm because of the weight of the attacker's body rolling back bringing the arm with it.

Bill secures the cross body armlock. To add more power to the lock, Bill will arch his hips as he pulls the arm to his chin. Also notice that Bill's head is up and off the mat. This gives added leverage to the move and enables the attacking wrestler to see what is going on.

Leg Jam Cross Body Armlock

The bottom wrestler, Steve, has found himself on his back and has jammed his right leg across his opponent's mid-section. Steve's right knee is on the outside at Bill's left hip and Steve's right foot is on the inside at Bill's right hip. This position can give Steve some space to get away.

Steve rolls to his right hip, keeping his right leg jammed against Bill's mid-section. Steve also traps Bill's right arm as shown in the photo. Steve will slightly shrimp to his right side.

Steve pushes a bit against Bill's midsection with his right leg to create some space and as he does this, he hooks his left leg over Bill's head and neck. All the while, Steve hugs Bill's right arm into his chest. Steve also continues to roll to his right.

Steve hooks Bill's head very hard with his left leg, making sure to point his toe to gain extra power. Steve also jams his right leg hard into Bill's midsection as shown in the photo. Steve starts to arch his hips and pull tightly on Bill's arm making sure it is planted firmly on his chest.

Steve rolls to his right as he arches his hips and straightens Bill's arm. Notice that Steve's left leg is hooked hard and tight around Bill's head and his right lower leg is jammed firmly in Bill's midsection. As Steve arches his hips and straightens Bill's arm, the armlock is secured.

Scissors Cross Body Armlock

This application is useful when you are holding your opponent and he attempts to escape by scissoring your leg. Although the hold is still valid, he may use the scissors to start his escape. This is also a great armlock to apply when your time for your hold has expired and you must work for a submission.

The bottom wrestler has hooked his legs in a scissors on the top man's right leg.

Steve, on top, now sits up a bit to give himself room to maneuver. Steve's left knee is on the mat at this point. The top wrestler may have to draw his right leg back a bit from the scissor. At this point, the bottom wrestler, Bill, still probably thinks Steve is simply trying to pull his trapped leg free. Notice that Steve is starting to trap Bill's right arm to his chest.

Steve quickly gets to a squatting position as shown and firmly traps Bill's right arm to his chest. It is important that the top wrestler squat and get off of his knee at this point.

Steve kicks his left leg over Bill's head and actually sits on Bill, all the while pulling the arm tighter to his chest.

Steve quickly rolls back to secure the cross body armlock. The bottom wrestler still has the right leg trapped, but it doesn't matter at this point. Also, notice how Steve has trapped Bill's head with his left leg, grabs Bill's arm like a baseball bat and pulls the fist to his chin to make sure his opponent taps out.

Head Roll Cross Body Armlock

This is one of the most popular applications of the cross body armlock used in any style of grappling. There are several variations of this move, but the one presented here is the one I have seen used most often and the one I teach my athletes. This is a fluid, athletic application of the cross body armlock and it's recommended that you make it part of your arsenal.

Bill, the top wrestler, positions himself behind Eric. Bill keeps his hands on Eric to feel any shift in his body movement.

Bill quickly digs his left foot into Eric's crotch area. Notice that Bill is coming from Eric's right side and that Bill's left upper leg is across Eric's low back.

Bill hooks his left leg around Eric's left side. The leg is wrapped tightly along the line of Eric's belt. The right leg is adding a pinching action across the body. Eric's body is controlled by the squeezing action of the legs. Bill's weight is centered over Eric's body at this point. Bill has posted with his left arm for stability.

Bill has posted with his head and has hooked Eric's near arm (in this case the left) with his right arm. Notice that Bill has placed his left leg at Eric's hip and is in the process of swinging his right leg over Eric's body.

Bill now has his right leg over Eric's body and (briefly) places his right knee on the mat. Bill continues to pull Eric's arm tightly to his chest. An important point here is that Bill's body is round and in a ball and he is rolling over his own right shoulder.

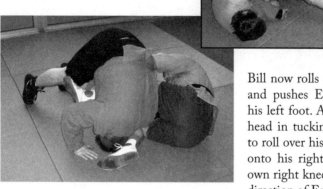

Bill now rolls onto his right side and pushes Eric's head in with his left foot. As Bill drives Eric's head in tucking it, it forces him to roll over his head. As Bill rolls onto his right side and hip, his own right knee is pointing in the direction of Eric's feet.

This photo shows that Bill has rolled Eric over and has assisted the whole move by hooking Eric's near leg (Eric's left leg) with his left arm. It is important to mention that this whole sequence of action is explosive and continuous.

Bill has rolled Eric over his head and onto his back. Notice that Bill has grabbed Eric's near leg with his left hand at the knee to assist in the rolling action.

Another view of the finish position after the roll. Bill makes sure to trap Eric's near arm tightly to his chest.

Bill secures the armlock by rolling back and arching his hips.

Crawl Up Arm and Belly Down Armlock

This application of the cross body armlock isn't fancy, but it works very well. Bill is behind Eric in a ride position and starts the move by grabbing Eric's left sleeve at the elbow.

Bill moves up Eric's body and starts to jam his left foot in Eric's left hip and crotch area. All the while, Bill keeps control of Eric's left elbow as shown.

Bill has firmly jammed his left foot in Eric's left hip and now hooks under Eric's left arm with his own left arm. Notice that Bill is driving his right forearm on the back of Eric's neck to soften him up and make Eric think he is going for a quarter nelson.

Bill continues to hook under Eric's left arm as he works his way up Eric's back.

Bill moves slightly to his left, all the while dragging Eric's left arm with him. Notice that Bill is starting to move his right leg up and will use it to hook over Eric's head. Bill has posted with his right hand for stability at Eric's head, and is using this to jam into Eric's head to cause discomfort.

Bill has moved a bit more to his left and has the room to hook over Eric's head with his right leg as shown. All the while, Bill continues to pull Eric's arm with his left arm. Also notice that Bill has posted out a bit more with his own right arm for stability.

Bill arches forcefully with his hips and hugs Eric's arm to his chest with both hands. Bill is posting on his head at this point which gives himself more room to arch with his hips. Notice that Bill's right leg is firmly hooked under Eric's head. This is a strong application of the cross body armlock.

Armlocks from Hold-downs

The rules of the sport of sambo are clear in that after a wrestler has held his opponent for the required time and accumulated points for the hold-down, he must actively attempt to secure a submission hold. If the top wrestler were to simply let his opponent up, it would be considered passivity. The object of hold-downs in sambo is to immobilize an opponent long enough to secure some type of submission technique.

Head and Arm Hold to the Straight Armlock

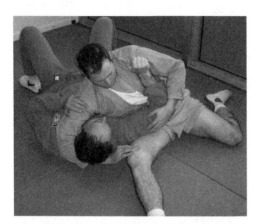

Shawn has Steve in a head and arm hold and has accumulated his 4 points. Now, he wants to secure a submission.

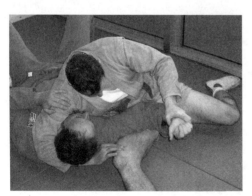

Shawn quickly grabs Steve's right arm at the wrist and bends it up and out. At this point, Shawn also starts to raise his left leg a bit.

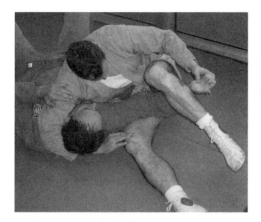

Shawn lets go of Steve's arm just long enough to loop his left leg over the outstretched arm.

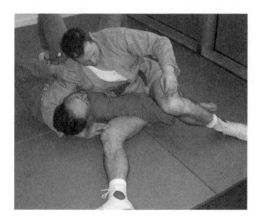

Shawn drives down on Steve's outstretched arm with his left knee. Shawn may slightly turn his left hip into the direction of the outstretched arm to add more pressure to the armlock.

Chest Hold to Upward Bent Armlock

Steve, on top, has secured a chest hold. The bottom wrestler, Eric, has broken the chest contact and is attempting to escape.

Steve plants his left elbow firmly against Eric's head and neck and as he does, he scoops Eric's arm up toward him by grabbing the elbow as shown.

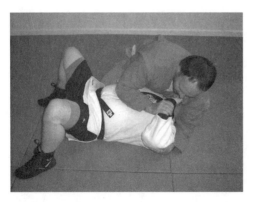

Steve keeps his elbow in the side of Eric's neck and hooks under Eric's upper arm. He also grabs Eric's wrist with his right hand. The hand position is important and if Steve were to extend his right thumb, it would point at himself. Steve starts pushing Eric's wrist upward in the same direction Eric's head is pointing.

Steve has let go of Eric's elbow with his left hand, but the elbow stays firmly jammed in the side of Eric's neck. Steve now firmly pushes Eric's wrist upward as shown.

Steve keeps his left elbow jammed in the side of Eric's neck as he grabs Eric's wrist with his left hand. Important: Steve does not plant Eric's wrist on the mat. He lifts it and makes room for his right arm to come under Eric's arm to secure the figure 4 lock that will be seen in the next photo.

Steve grabs his left wrist with his right hand and bends Eric's elbow up and inward. Steve does not let Eric's left wrist rest on the mat as this stops the pressure and lessens the leverage exerted in the armlock.

Chest Hold to Downward Bent Armlock

As before, Steve has secured a chest hold and Eric is attempting to escape. Steve has scooped under Eric's left arm and is pulling it toward his chest. Steve has also grabbed Eric's wrist with his left hand.

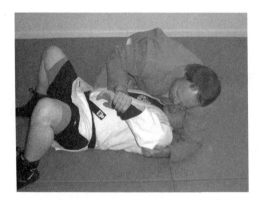

Steve continues to scoop up on Eric's left elbow and now firmly drives Eric's left arm downward as shown.

Steve has a firm grasp of Eric's wrist with his left hand and is hooking under Eric's arm with his left arm as shown.

Steve has grabbed his right wrist with his left hand and has completed the figure 4.

To apply pressure, Steve lifts up with his left forearm and draws Eric's arm in with his right hand. If Eric is very strong or flexible, Steve can roll or shift his weight toward the same direction Eric's head is pointed for more leverage.

Upper Chest Hold to the Cross Body Armlock

This is a popular and effective hold/armlock combination and can be used in all styles of grappling.

The top wrestler, Bill, moves to his right side and over Eric's right shoulder as shown in the photo. Bill continues to keep the chest contact with his opponent so the hold stays in effect.

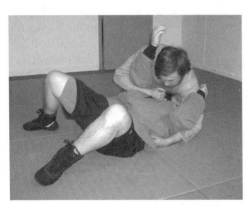

At this point, Bill hooks under Eric's right arm with his right arm as shown. Bill also will raise up a bit to allow more freedom of movement for himself.

Bill quickly moves to his right as he continues to hook Eric's arm close to his chest. Notice that Bill has jumped up into a squat position and is careful to keep his body and hips very close to Eric's. Bill also has wedged his right knee very hard in Eric's rib cage.

Bill now is curled up and over Eric's body, as shown in the photo. Bill steps over Eric's head with his left foot. Notice that Bill has had to post with his left hand for stability. The top wrestler must move efficiently and quickly to secure this position.

Bill quickly rolls back and drags Eric's arm with him as he does. Notice that Bill's right shin is firmly jammed in Eric's side and rib cage. Bill has also trapped Eric's head by hooking his left heel firmly in the side of Eric's neck. To secure the armlock, Bill rolls back and arches his hips as he pulls on Eric's arm.

Arm Levers to Pry the Opponent's Arm Free

Once you get your opponent on his back and in the leg press position, he will certainly know he's in trouble and immediately grab his arms instinctively to protect them. What have come to be called "levers" are the methods we use to straighten out his arm and get him to submit. I have included some of my favorites. They are my favorite because I have observed these to be the levers that have the highest ratio of success in actual competition.

Thigh Lever

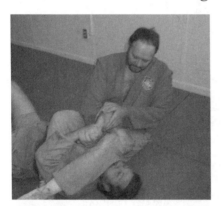

Steve, on top, hooks under Bill's near arm with his right arm as shown, making sure to firmly grasp his own thigh. Steve is in a strong leg press position.

Steve rolls to his left (in the direction Bill's head is pointing) and continues to apply pressure on Bill's near arm with his right forearm. Steve is letting the weight of his own body assist him as he rolls. Steve keeps his strong leg press position.

The weight of Steve's body and the rolling action, along with constant pressure from pulling on Bill's near arm causes the bottom wrestler to loosen his grasp.

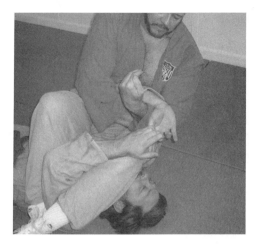

Often, it's helpful for the top wrestler to hook under the bottom man's near arm with his left hand as shown. Make sure to scoop with the palm up, giving you more power as you hook under his arm.

Hooking under the bottom wrestler's arm and pulling it into your own chest will loosen his grasp quickly. Steve, the top wrestler, may have to use jerking motions to loosen the arm if Bill is too strong.

Steve rolls into a cross body armlock after levering the arm free.

Arm and Leg Lever

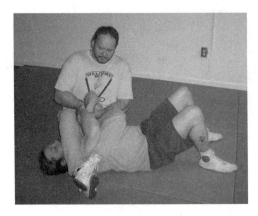

The top wrestler has his opponent in the leg press position. This lever is very effective and is used in sambo, judo and mixed martial arts.

The top wrestler rolls to his left side (closest to his opponent's legs) and hooks under his opponent's near arm with his right and starts to pry it loose using his own thigh as shown.

The top wrestler has grasped his hands together and pulled his opponent's leg even closer to his chest. He constantly pulls his opponent's arm and leg to him. Notice that the top wrestler is attempting to bring his opponent's knee to his own head. Doing this gets you in the right position to secure the lever.

The top wrestler continues to roll to his left side (toward the bottom wrestler's legs) as he traps the near leg and grasps his hands together. At this point, the top wrestler hooks his left leg over his opponent's head and neck. Notice that the toe is pointed to add extra power into the hooking motion on the head.

The top wrestler has forcefully hooked his opponent's head and loosened the bottom wrestler's grip. The top wrestler has also levered his opponent's arm free and starts to arch his hips as he rolls a bit more to his right side. Notice that the top wrestler keeps a strong hold on the opponent's leg.

At left is the finish position. The top wrestler has trapped the bottom wrestler's leg and arm and is arching his hips to add pressure to the bottom man's elbow. The angle of this position along with the pressure from the hips being arched into the elbow causes a quick submission.

Here is another view of the finish position.

Lapel Grab Lever

The top wrestler has secured a leg press position and hooks under his opponent's arm with his right hand (the one closest to the opponent's legs). He hooks the arm deep and wedges the opponent's arm in the crook of his elbow.

At left, the top wrestler grabs his own lapel with his right hand and starts to roll toward his opponent's head. The top wrestler makes sure to pull his opponent's arm tightly to his chest.

The top wrestler now starts to roll hard to his left (toward the opponent's head) and upward with his elbow as he pulls the opponent's arm in the direction of his roll (toward the opponent's head).

The top wrestler quickly snatches the opponent's arm with his own left hand and rolls hard to his left. As he does this, the top wrestler keeps pulling the arm into his own chest to allow his body weight to help in levering the arm free.

The top wrestler then rolls back into a cross body armlock to get the submission.

Bent Armlock (Up Position)

The top wrestler, Steve, pushes the far arm toward the mat. He is positioned on a stable base. Steve firmly grasps Bill's left arm as shown.

Steve has stabilized Bill's wrist by grabbing it with his left hand and now will reach under the arm with his right arm to grab his own wrist as shown. Notice that Steve has jammed his left elbow directly into the side of Bill's neck as he places his forearm on the mat. This action diverts Bill's attention from his wrist and arm and focuses it on his head and neck discomfort. Doing this also helps Steve to provide a base for his armlock. Steve does not place Bill's wrist on the mat, rather, he keeps it slightly off the mat.

Steve grabs his own wrist in a figure 4 hold and lifts up on Bill's elbow as he slightly pulls the bottom wrestler's wrist in toward the head. Steve may shift his weight forward in the direction of Bill's head to gain more leverage. Steve shifts his weight toward Bill's wrist.

Another view of the bent armlock is shown here. Notice the top wrestler's angle in relation to his opponent.

Bent Armlock (Down Position)

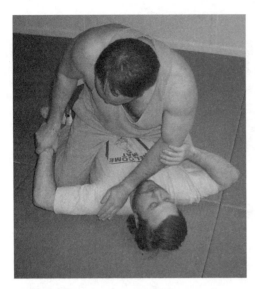

Steve, on top, is astride Bill as shown. Steve initiates the armlock by grasping Bill's left wrist and pushing it downward in the direction of his knee and toward the mat.

Steve has a firm grasp on Bill's wrist and pushes it to the mat. Steve continues to scoop up on the bottom wrestler's elbow and upper arm as shown. Steve makes sure he maintains a strong base with his legs and can also start to roll toward Bill's head to exert some more control.

Steve grabs his right wrist with his left hand as shown in a figure 4 hold. Notice that Steve's left arm is under Bill's left shoulder. Steve lifts Bill's elbow off the mat with his left arm which causes pain in the elbow and shoulder.

Rolling Bent Armlock

Steve has applied the bent arm-lock in the downward position as shown at left. If the bottom wrestler is very strong, he might be able to start to sit up on his buttocks to initiate an escape or relieve the pressure of the arm-lock.

Steve, on top, keeps his figure 4 hold on Bill's elbow maintaining his control with the armlock. Steve also lifts his left leg and hooks it over Bill's head as shown in the photo.

Steve quickly rolls over his right shoulder, all the while maintaining his control with the armlock. Notice that Steve hooks his left leg hard over Bill's head as he rolls. It is important for Steve to stay as round as possible and not flatten out with his body as he rolls over his right shoulder.

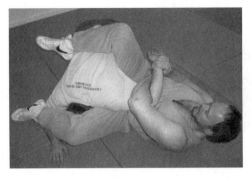

Steve has rolled Bill over onto Bill's front side. Steve has hooked his left leg over Bill's head and neck, making sure to point his toe for more power in the leg. Steve has also wrapped his right leg over Bill's back as shown. Steve clamps the bent armlock on tightly at this point hugging Bill's left elbow to his body and driving Bill's wrist upward toward the ceiling.

Here is another view of the above photo. Steve's legs control Bill's body at this point as the bent armlock is applied. This is an unusual application of the bent armlock, but is effective on an opponent who is very strong. The rolling action gives momentum to the application of the armlock.

Bent Armlock from the Bottom

The top wrestler, Bill, has pushed Steve's left knee to the mat and is attempting to get past Steve's legs to apply a hold down. Steve quickly grabs Bill's right wrist with his left hand as shown.

Steve rolls to his left hip and side all the while continuing to grasp Bill's right wrist firmly with his left hand. Notice that Steve is not on his back, but rather on his left buttocks. Steve also his right arm over Bill's right shoulder and is about to grab his own wrist.

Steve grabs his own left wrist with his right hand in a keylock hold making sure to hug Bill's right shoulder tight to his body. Steve is still laying on his left hip and side as shown.

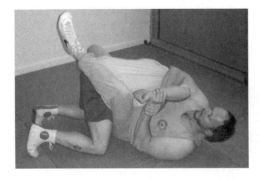

Steve quickly rolls onto his back as he hugs Bill's trapped arm to his body. Steve spins to his right as he places his left leg over Bill's back. This action also causes the top wrestler, Bill, to be driven forward onto his head and face.

Notice Steve's bottom leg, in this case the right leg, under Bill's torso. Steve pinches his bottom leg and top leg together as much as possible, trapping the top wrestler and preventing him from moving. As Steve does this, he drives Bill's wrist upward toward the ceiling and hugs Bill's elbow to his body causing pain in the elbow and shoulder.

This application of the bent armlock is a good way to turn the table on your opponent who has the top position.

Shoulder Lever Bent Armlock

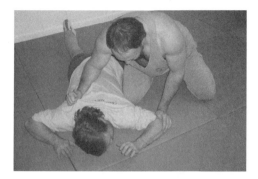

This is an unusual armlock that can take your opponent by surprise. Bill, on the bottom, is flat on his front in the chicken position and Steve controls him as shown. Steve traps Bill's left elbow on the mat with his left hand.

Steve jams his left knee into Bill's left armpit and he grasps Bill's left wrist with his right hand. Steve also makes sure to grab Bill's wrist palm up and wedge his arm across Bill's shoulder and upper arm.

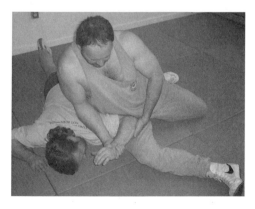

Steve sits through with his right leg and is careful to jam his right hip into Bill's left armpit. As he does this, Steve lifts up on Bill's wrist and elbow, pulling Bill's elbow tightly into Steve's right hip. Steve wedges his right elbow firmly on Bill's shoulder as shown. This provides a good lever and causes some discomfort to his opponent.

Steve grasps Bill's left wrist with both of his hands palm up as shown in the photo. Steve pulls Bill's wrist upward toward the ceiling. Steve continues to drive his left elbow and forearm across Bill's upper arm and keeps Bill's left elbow tight in Steve's own right hip. This action causes the elbow joint to bend backward causing pain in the joint.

Here is another view of the above photograph showing the armlock being applied. Notice that Steve, on top, is leaning into Bill's body as he levers Bill's wrist upward causing pain in the elbow joint as well as shoulder.

Sit-through Straight Armlock

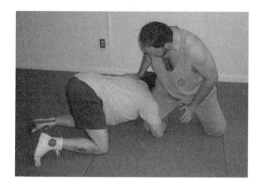

Bill has attempted a single leg attack or a switch and has made the mistake of not controlling the top wrestler's leg well enough.

Steve, the top wrestler, quickly jams his right elbow into Bill's right armpit and starts to sit through with his right leg.

Steve sits through with his right leg and positions himself on his right hip as he grasps Bill's right wrist with his left hand as shown. Steve also keeps his right elbow jammed in Bill's armpit.

Steve pulls Bill's arm straight and clasps his right elbow tightly on Bill's upper right triceps. Steve pulls Bill's arm into his ribs and leans heavily on Bill's upper arm and shoulder area. Notice that Steve is driving into Bill's body with his feet. As Steve pulls on his opponent's arm and leans into him wedging the elbow into his own rib cage area, pain is caused on Bill's elbow and shoulder.

If the bottom wrestler collapses flat onto his front side as shown in this photo, the top wrestler can exert even more pressure on the elbow and shoulder. Notice how Steve, the top wrestler, is pulling Bill's arm forcefully and driving into his opponent with his feet.

2-on-1 Front Takedown to the Straight Armlock

This is an effective way to pick up some points taking your opponent to the mat as well as securing an armlock. Chris, the wrestler on the left has gripped with his opponent, Bob.

Chris shucks Bob's right arm off of his shoulder as shown and moves closer to him. Notice that Chris is leading with his left foot and his weight is evenly distributed for optimal balance.

Chris quickly scoops under Bob's right arm with his right hand (palm up). Chris' left hand is hooking under Bob's right shoulder. Chris is also driving his right shoulder into Bob as shown. Chris has his head down at this point. Notice the position of Chris' body and feet.

Chris uses both of his hands to hook under Bob's right arm. Chris continues to drive into his opponent as he scoops Bob's arms into his upper chest. Notice how Chris is driving with his legs into his opponent.

Chris quickly wraps his left arm around Bob's waist and grabs Bob's far (left) hip. Chris continues to scoop Bob's right arm into his chest and really starts to drive Bob's upper body down toward the mat.

Chris places his left leg inside Bob's right leg as shown. Notice how close Chris' left foot is to Bob's right foot. Chris continues to drive Bob's upper body down toward the mat. Chris uses his left leg and foot to trip his opponent forward.

Chris drives Bob forward and downward to the mat, continuing to hold onto Bob's far (left) hip. Chris is using his left shoulder to help drive his opponent to the mat. Chris makes sure to continue to scoop Bob's right arm to his chest as he drives forward.

Chris immediately sits through with his left leg as shown and scoops Bob's right arm into his armpit. As Chris does this, he makes sure to grab Bob's forearm with his hands palm up. Grasping with the hands in the palm up position gives the top wrestler more control and strength.

Chris secures the submission by pulling Bob's right arm into his ribcage and pulls out on Bob's wrist with both of his hands. Chris makes sure to keep his right hip firmly wedged in Bob's armpit. Chris also drives with his back (right) leg and he continues to sit through. This secures the armlock causing pressure on both the elbow and shoulder.

SECTION FOUR:
Leg Submissions

"Do simple things with consistent excellence rather than complicated things done poorly."
Vince Lombardi

The sport of sambo is where effective and realistic leg submissions were born. The Soviets focused in on this unique aspect of groundfighting and made leglocks a major part of sambo. This section looks at the leg submissions that have been used with regularity and with a high ratio of success in actual sambo matches.

It is important to remember that when doing leg submissions, you must stick to the core skills and develop variations that will work for you. If you try to get too fancy or go for moves that are complicated with a lot of steps to them, your chances of securing the leg submission are lessened. If you do simple things with consistent excellence rather than complicated things done poorly, your chances of success improve dramatically. This is true with any aspect of sambo and is especially true with leg submissions. My goal is to show you leg submissions that really work and have a high ratio of success in competitive situations. These submissions can be applied to any form of grappling, whether it be sambo, sport jujitsu or mixed martial arts. Jimmy Martin, the Pan American Games Champion, once told me his cardinal rule for effective leglocks was to follow the KISS method..."Keep It Simple Stupid." I don't want to call anyone stupid, but you get what I mean.

Also, it is very important that when a leg submission has been applied on you, make sure you tap out or yell out to signal that you have submitted before there is too much pain. It has been my experience that the legs aren't as sensitive to pain as the arms are and damage is usually done on the knee or ankle joints before the pain signals reach the brain. If your opponent has secured the leg or ankle lock and there is no way out, remember the old adage "when in doubt, tap out." This will save your legs to fight another day.

As with any aspect of sambo groundfighting, position is fundamental to effective leg submissions. You must gain a good position, then methodically work to establish control over your opponent's lower body. Immediately go for the ankle or knee lock after getting control of your opponent's lower body and aggressively work for the submission. Sometimes leg submissions take time to set up and you have to have a strong ride position to dominate your opponent or at least keep him from moving too quickly or getting away from you.

In my experience, the most commonly used leg submissions are ankle locks. While this is a basic, straight-forward approach to making an opponent tap out, ankle locks are highly effective and have a good ratio of success. They aren't flashy or complicated, but they work!

However, the cross body knee lock is effective as well and the near leg ride bent knee lock has been used often in world-class sambo events with good results.

As said previously, follow the KISS approach to applying leg submissions. Keep it simple and make it work. If you try to get too complicated or fancy, your opponent will have time to escape or counter.

Remember, you don't score style points in sambo. Sometimes seeing two sambo wrestlers scramble for the dominant position to work a leg submission looks almost humorous, but if successful, the end result is getting an opponent to tap out. Don't hesitate to take any of the moves shown here and make them work for you.

Core Skills of Leglocks

The legs on a human body are stronger than the arms, and as a result, it is vital that you control your opponent's lower extremities as much as possible before securing the leg or ankle lock. However, there are those occasions when you immediately go for the ankle and completely surprise your opponent and get a quick submission, but the rule of thumb is to focus in on his leg, control it, then apply the lock.

There are two basic areas we attack in leg submissions. They are the ankle and the knee. From my experience, the most often-used leg submissions are the ankle locks. Always lock the ankle in a straight line with the leg and don't twist the ankle. Heel hooks, toe holds and other submission holds of this type are all excellent skills, but the chance of doing severe and permanent damage is very high and this is why these moves are illegal in sambo competition today. The knee locks can be applied with the knee straight or the knee bent. As long as there is no twisting of the joint, both the straight knee locks and the bent knee locks are allowed in sambo matches.

Feet Under the Buttocks and Squeeze the Knees Together

When applying an ankle lock, trap your opponent's leg and make sure to keep your feet under his buttocks as shown. This gives the attacking wrestler a great deal of control and protects his own ankles from being attacked.

Cradling the Ankle in the Armpit

This photo shows how to cradle your opponent's foot in your armpit to gain maximum control of the ankle. Notice that Shawn, the attacking wrestler, has his opponent's shoelaces in his armpit and the top of the foot is nestled in the back of the armpit as well. This photo also shows another view of how to pinch or squeeze the knees together and how to jam your feet under your opponent's buttocks for control of his leg.

Scissoring Opponent's Leg

A common method of controlling your opponent's leg when doing ankle locks is to scissor the leg. I don't advocate this as it gives your opponent a chance to attack your ankles too easily. While this method of controlling the leg can be effective, you will have every bit as much control by keeping your feet under your opponent's buttocks and pinching your knees together.

Who Has Who Situation

Often, when a wrestler scissors his opponent's leg when doing an ankle lock, his opponent will counter with an ankle lock of his own. This is what we call the "who has who situation" and is a big reason why scissoring your opponent's leg is not an effective means of control.

Ankle Lock Defense

Defend against the ankle lock by shoving your ankle as hard as you can through your attacker's arm (above) and pulling on both of his lapels. Make sure to aim with your heel and keep driving your leg as far as you can forward. Pulling on the attacker's lapels is important as this keeps him from rolling back to secure the ankle lock. Your goal is to keep him from positioning your ankle in his arms for the lock and to keep him from rolling back to gain leverage or rolling you in a gator roll.

The Gator Roll

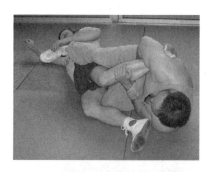

Much like an alligator rolls with his victim, roll to secure the ankle lock if your opponent starts to move out of the hold. As you roll, continually cinch the ankle in tighter. Rolling an opponent over in the gator roll has a good ratio of success in securing the submission.

At left, Steve, the wrestler applying the ankle lock, rolls over and will continue to roll, all the while cinching up on the ankle to make the hold tighter. Sometimes, you may have to roll several times to tighten the ankle lock.

131

Trapping the Leg

The legs are very strong, so it is important to trap your opponent's leg or foot effectively before securing the leg submission. Isolate the leg or foot you are attacking, then aggressively attempt the leg submission. Knowing how to "leg wrestle" (left) is a skill every sambo wrestler should master.

Here is another example of how a wrestler should quickly attempt to trap and control his opponent's leg or foot. While armlocks are effective, a sambo wrestler should not forget to aggressively tie up his opponent's legs and lower body and try to secure a leg submission. Key in on the body part you want to control, then go for the submission. Sometimes you can surprise your opponent by quickly slapping on an ankle lock after a throw or takedown.

Straight Ankle Lock

Don't take this technique for granted. This is the leg submission that is used most often. Compare it to a boxer's jab. If you've ever boxed, you know that your primary punch is your jab. A good sambo wrestler's primary leg submission is the ankle lock. Master this move and you will quickly learn the other leg submissions.

 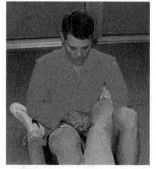

The two most common hand and arm control positions of the ankle are shown above. The hands are clasped together in a "square" lock in the photo at right and the hands are controlling the opponent's ankle in a keylock grasp on the left.

Roll Back to the Ankle Lock

After you have taken your opponent to the mat or secured his ankle, quickly cradle his ankle in your armpit as shown and pull his leg into your crotch. If possible, be in a squatting position and immediately roll back, all the while pulling on his leg and ankle. Don't reach back with your arm. Roll backward and arch your hips forcefully.

Squeeze your knees together to clamp your opponent's leg tightly and keep your feet under his buttocks. By keeping your feet under his buttocks, you don't give him a chance to grab your own ankle as a counter to your ankle lock. Lean back and arch your hips and this will cause a quick tap out.

Between Legs Chest Hold to the Ankle Lock

Steve has secured the Between Legs Chest Hold. He realizes that he can't end the match by holding his opponent to the mat (as in wrestling or judo), so he must keep chest contact as long as possible to get the maximum points allowed.

Bill, on bottom, breaks chest contact with Steve and attempts to either push him away and off of him to create space so he can further escape or attempt a spinning cross body armlock as a counter. Bill may try to roll Steve over and gain the top position. Steve now either has to try to regain his chest hold position or switch to a submission technique.

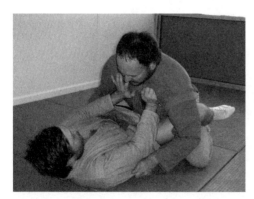

Here is another view of the above photo. Notice that Bill is starting to bring his knees up so that he can use them to wedge against Steve's body to create more space or to attempt to control Steve's body for a counter technique.

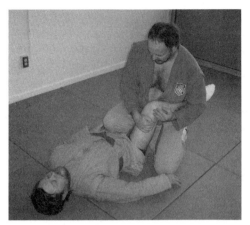

Steve wedges his right knee hard between Bill's legs. As he does this, he hugs Bill's leg to his rib cage. Notice that Steve uses both of his hands to pull Bill's leg to his rib cage. Doing this, traps Bill's leg to Steve's body where he can more easily roll back into the ankle lock. Notice that Steve is on his other knee for stability. Make sure you wedge that knee in your opponent's crotch firmly before rolling back to secure the ankle.

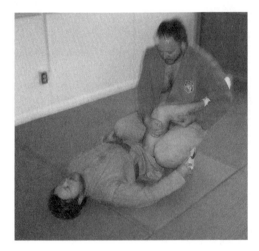

Steve quickly jumps into a squatting position as shown. When you squat, makes sure to be as close as possible to your opponent. Notice that Steve has started to squeeze his knees together which controls Bill's leg.

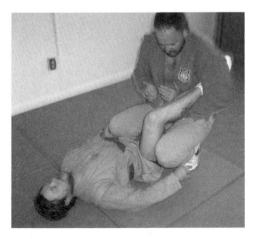

Now that he has trapped his opponent's lower body, Steve starts to secure the ankle lock with his hands. Steve starts to slide his left arm back onto Bill's foot more tightly as he clasps his hands together.

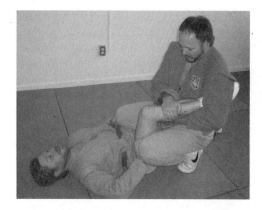

Steve has now gained control of Bill's ankle with his hands and starts to roll back to apply pressure to the ankle.

Steve has rolled back, applying pressure on the ankle as he does. The top wrestler uses the weight of his own body to add momentum and leverage to the ankle lock. Often, it is useful to arch with the hips as well to add more leverage to the ankle lock.

Belly Down Ankle Lock

This is a common way to secure an ankle lock in sambo. Steve, the top wrestler, is riding his opponent and has snatched Bill's left ankle.

Steve breaks Bill down flat onto his front by snatching Bill's left ankle as shown. Notice how Steve uses his head and left shoulder to drive his opponent onto his front and flat in the chicken position.

Steve quickly turns to Bill's feet as he continues to pull up on Bill's left leg.

Steve cradles Bill's ankle in his armpit as shown in the photo at left and has posted his hand for stability as he starts to swing his left leg over Bill's body.

As Steve swings his left leg over Bill's flat body, he immediately grasps his hands in a figure 4 hold on Bill's ankle.

Steve drives forward onto his head as he arches his hips and secures the ankle lock on his opponent. Notice that Steve is posting on his head for stability. Doing this also gives him room to arch his hips. If Steve were to lay flat on his face, he would not be able to arch his hips very well. The hip arch adds greatly to the effect of the ankle lock.

Gator Roll Ankle Lock

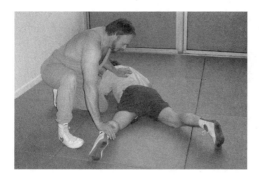

The rolling ankle lock is often called the "gator roll" or "crocodile roll" in many sambo clubs. Steve, the top wrestler, is to the side of his opponent who is flat on his front.

Steve quickly swings his leg over his opponent, Bill, and places his body in the opposite direction of his opponent.

Steve immediately grabs Bill's left ankle and cradles it in his armpit. Steve posts with his left hand for stability.

Steve quickly applies a figure 4 hold on Bill's left ankle and immediately starts to roll to his left side.

Steve continues to roll as he applies pressure on Bill's ankle. This rolling action helps greatly in cinching the ankle lock tighter. Steve may have to roll more than once, continually gaining pressure on Bill's ankle as he rolls. Often, the opponent will tap out during the course of a roll and the referee must be close to the action to stop the wrestler from rolling any more which might cause damage to his opponent.

Steve has rolled Bill and makes sure to keep his feet under Bill's buttocks. Doing this keeps Steve's ankles away from Bill's grasp, as Bill will try to grab Steve's ankle as a counter ankle lock during the course of this entire movement.

Cross Body Knee Lock

The cross body knee lock is a move that can be quickly applied and uses the momentum of the attacker's rolling action into the move to make it work effectively. This knee lock is a good submission to follow-through with after a throw or takedown. Think of this as the lower body's version of the cross body armlock.

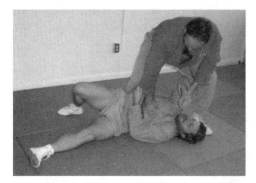

This sequence shows how this leglock can be applied as a follow through technique from a throw or takedown. Steve, the top wrestler, has just thrown Bill and wants to secure the cross body leglock.

Steve quickly shifts his body toward the direction of Bill's leg nearest him.

Steve scoops Bill's near leg (in this case Bill's right leg) with his right hand under the knee as shown. As Steve does this, he starts to crouch low and move his left leg close to Bill.

Steve traps Bill's right leg to his chest firmly as he wedges his left leg through Bill's legs. Steve will now roll to his left shoulder as he scoops the leg. This photo shows Steve posting with his left hand, but it isn't necessary when you actually perform the move in a real situation. Allow the momentum of your body's weight to assist you in this rolling action.

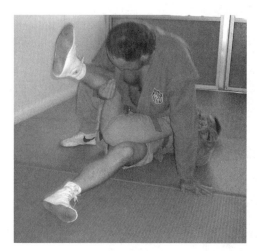

Here is another view of the action described above. Notice how Steve has pointed his left leg through and to his right. Doing this helps in the rolling action required to secure a strong leglock. Also notice how Steve has scooped or hooked under Bill's leg. Steve has his palm up for added power in the scooping action.

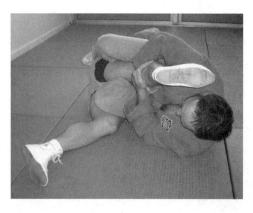

Steve has rolled to his left shoulder, all the while hugging Bill's leg to his chest. Notice that Steve has placed his right foot on Bill's buttocks and is arching with his hips to gain added leverage in the knee lock. This submission "bars" the knee, which is another way of saying that is straightens the knee causing pain in the joint.

Outside Roll to Cross Body Knee Lock

The top wrestler, Chris, scoops under Bob's right leg and hugs it close to his chest. As he does this, Chris jams his right shin and knee between Bob's legs in the crotch.

Chris rotates, turning his right shoulder and he rolls to his right on the outside of Bob's body. As he dos this, Chris hugs Bob's right leg tightly to his chest and grasps the leg with both hands. Chris is rolling to his right with his right shin jammed in Bob's right hip.

Chris has completed his roll and lands on his right hip as he arches with his hips for leverage. Notice that Chris has also hooked his left foot just below Bob's left knee. This is an effective knee lock when the top wrestler is between his opponent's legs initially.

Knee Jam Bent Knee Lock

This is a simple bent knee submission. It's one of those situations that presents itself and if you think to take advantage of it, you can come up with an unexpected victory. Basically, you jam your knee into the inside of your opponent's knee and create a wedge as you pull up on his leg. This is an old leg submission and one of the first I learned in sambo. Start by getting a good ride position as shown.

Chris, the top wrestler, started his ride position by snatching the bottom wrestler's near (left) ankle. Chris starts to drive Bob, the bottom wrestler, toward Bob's head with his left arm across the back as shown. Chris also scoops up harder on Bob's near ankle. This scooping of the near ankle helps break Bob down as well as set up the leglock that is to follow.

Chris has driven Bob flat onto his front and quickly starts to jam his left knee directly into the back of Bob's left knee. Also notice that Chris continues to pull up on Bob's left foot.

144

Chris is careful to keep his knee wedged into the back of Bob's knee joint and not let his left knee rest on the mat. Chris wants to use his left knee as wedge so the upcoming knee lock will be effective.

Chris has his left knee firmly jammed in the back of Bob's knee and is leaning back heavily on his opponent. Notice that Chris has grabbed Bob's foot at the shoe-laces as he pulls back on the foot. This gives Chris more control of the whole foot and lower leg.

This photo shows another method of grasping the hands to secure the ankle lock. Rather than grabbing the foot on the shoe laces as shown above, the top wrestler can clasp his hands together in a "square" lock as shown here. Either method of grabbing your opponent's foot is good and it's a matter of preference which way you grab him.

Near Leg Ride Bent Knee Lock

Shawn, the top wrestler, has laced his left leg into Steve's near (left) leg as shown.

A close-up view of the above near leg ride is shown at left. Notice how Shawn has hooked his left foot over Steve's lower leg for control.

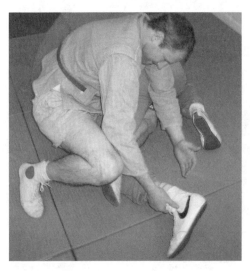

Shawn now reverses his direction and as he does, drives his elbow directly onto Steve's buttocks. Shawn keeps his left leg hooked tightly onto Steve's left leg for maximum control. By driving his elbow on Steve's buttocks, Shawn drives Steve forward and flat on his stomach, or at least off of a stable position.

Shawn can also figure 4 his own leg as shown in this photo for added pressure. This is a good option if you are not flexible enough to push on your foot with your other foot as shown in the above photo. This is a powerful leglock and popular in sambo.

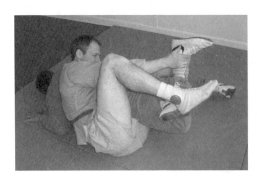

To finish the leglock, Shawn pulls Steve's foot up and toward Shawn's body in a direct line with Steve's upper leg. Shawn pushes on his left foot (the one wedged in Steve's near leg) with his right foot. Doing this adds great pressure to this bent knee lock.

Shawn grabs Steve's foot at the shoelaces and starts to pull up on the foot. Shawn's left leg is a wedge in Steve's near leg.

Cuban Leg Grab to Standing Ankle Lock

This is a good series showing how leg submissions can be used to follow through from a throw or takedown. This throw, the Cuban leg grab, is effective and used often in the sport of sambo.

To start, Shawn, on the left, has gripped Steve with his right hand around Steve's left arm and is gripping toward the middle of Steve's back.

Shawn shoots in with his right leg using a lunge step as he grabs the inside of Steve's leg just above the knee. Shawn also drives into Steve's body with his head for more leverage. Notice how Shawn has lowered his level by bending with his legs and not bending over at the waist.

Here is the back view of the previous photo. Notice how Shawn has trapped Steve's left arm with his right arm. Shawn's left elbow is tucked in and firmly attached to Steve's side. Doing this helps break the balance and gain momentum into the throw.

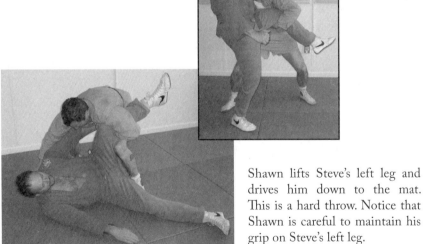

Shawn lifts Steve's left leg and drives him down to the mat. This is a hard throw. Notice that Shawn is careful to maintain his grip on Steve's left leg.

Shawn steps into Steve, pulling up and extending Steve's leg. Shawn traps the leg by pinching his knees together and jamming both his feet under Steve's buttocks and hip as shown. This is an effective standing ankle lock, but if your opponent starts to free himself, you can quickly squat and roll back to apply this ankle lock from the ground.

The photo at left shows how Shawn has squatted and started to roll back to secure the ankle lock. Notice that Shawn's feet are under Steve's buttocks which keeps Steve from grabbing Shawn's ankle for a counter ankle lock.

Shawn has completed his roll backward and secured the ankle lock. Shawn is arching his hips to add pressure to the ankle lock.

About the Author

Steve Scott started training in the sport of judo in 1965 and was introduced to sambo in 1976. He holds high rank in both Kodokan Judo and Shingitai Jujitsu and is a member of the United States Sombo Association's Hall of Fame. He is the head coach of the Welcome Mat Judo, Jujitsu and Sambo Club in Kansas City, Missouri. A graduate of the University of Missouri-Kansas City, he is the director of the community center where his sambo, judo and jujitsu training center is located. He is married to Becky Scott, an accomplished athlete in both sambo and judo and a World and Pan American Games Sambo Champion. Not surprisingly, the Scotts met at a judo tournament.

Starting his own club in 1969, Steve initially taught judo and jujitsu, then added sambo in 1976. His passion is teaching and he has trained thousands of people and promoted hundreds of tournaments in judo, sambo and sport jujitsu.

Steve has personally coached 3 World Champions, 2 Pan American Games Champions and 58 National AAU Champions in the sport of sambo. He has also developed numerous judo champions at his Welcome Mat training center, including a member of the 1996 U.S. Olympic Judo Team, almost 100 individual athletes who have won National Judo Championships and numerous athletes who have been members of official U.S. teams in international competition including the Word Championships, Pan American Championships, World University Games and other events. As an athlete, Steve competed in several AAU Sambo Nationals, winning gold twice and bronze once. He also won numerous regional and state sambo championships in the Midwest.

He served as the official U.S. Team Coach at the 1983 Pan American Games, where his women's team won four gold medals and six silver medals, winning the team championship. This was the only time sambo was admitted as a sport in the quadrennial Pan American Games. Steve has also coached at the World Sombo Championships and at the World (under-21) Judo Championships on different occasions. He has trained, competed and coached In North America, South America, Europe and Japan.

Steve was introduced to sambo by one of his judo coaches, Ken Regennitter, who suggested he try this rugged form of jacket wrestling because of his natural affinity for submission holds. In 1976, Steve met Dr. Ivan Olsen, the National Chairman for the Amateur Athletic Union's Sambo Committee, who became his mentor, as well as the mentor to many other sambo wrestlers and coaches.

Steve introduced sambo to the Midwest, when he promoted the first Missouri Valley AAU Sambo Championship in Kansas City, Missouri in 1977. He was one of the original founding members of the U.S. Sombo Association in 1985 and served as the Secretary for the National AAU Sambo Committee in the late 1970s and early 1980s. He also held the first National AAU Women's Sambo Championships in 1980 and the first National AAU Youth Sambo Championships, also in 1980.

Steve is the author of COACHING ON THE MAT and co-author (along with Bill West) of SECRETS OF THE CROSS BODY ARMLOCK and is featured on several videos currently on the market.

Index

straight armlock 26, 96–97, 121–124
submission techniques 9, 18, 29, 61, 62, 70, 74

T

takedown 76–77
tap out 70, 74, 127
the guard 30
thigh lever 104–105
throwing 18
toe holds 129
top ride position 27
top standing position 26
trapping the leg 132
turnovers 23, 34

U

United States 10, 16, 17, 18
United States Sombo Association 19
upper chest hold 65–66, 102
upright position 72
upward bent armlock 98–99

V

variations 127
vertical chest hold 66

W

weight distributed 65
who has who situation 130
World Sambo Championships 18
wrestler's ride 25

Also Available from Turtle Press:

Martial Arts Injury Care and Prevention
Timing for Martial Arts
Strength and Power Training
Complete Kickboxing
Ultimate Flexibility
Boxing: A 12 Week Course
The Fighter's Body: An Owner's Manual
The Science of Takedowns, Throws and Grappling for Self-defense
Fighting Science
Martial Arts Instructor's Desk Reference
Solo Training
Solo Training 2
Fighter's Fact Book
Conceptual Self-defense
Martial Arts After 40
Warrior Speed
The Martial Arts Training Diary for Kids
Teaching Martial Arts
Combat Strategy
The Art of Harmony
Total MindBody Training
1,001 Ways to Motivate Yourself and Others
Ultimate Fitness through Martial Arts
Taekwondo Kyorugi: Olympic Style Sparring

For more information:
Turtle Press
1-800-77-TURTL
e-mail: orders@turtlepress.com

http://www.turtlepress.com